Number Games and Activities for 0 - 10

BEV DUNBAR

Introduction

Here are ten easy-to-use, multi-purpose games to help make early number come alive in your classroom. This is a companion book to "Exploring 1-5" and "Exploring 6-10".

The ten themes have immediate appeal for young children, who will love manipulating frogs, dog bones and freckles as part of their daily Maths activities. And with ten activities, there's plenty for up to a whole class to use together, working in groups of three or more.

Each activity has been designed to help your children practise recognising, matching and using numbers 0-10 in an imaginative way, with follow-up ideas for using the numbers 11-19. To help you with your programming, there's a set of Outcome Indicators matched to each activity.

The activities relate to the following objectives in Reception Year/P1.
- Say and use the number names in order to familiar contexts.
- Count reliably up to ten everyday objects.
- Recognise numerals 1-9. Use language such as "more" or "less" to compare two numbers.
- Begin to use the vocabulary involved in adding and subtracting.

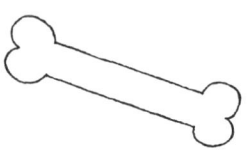

All you need to get yourself started is a small group of parent helpers to photocopy, colour, laminate and cut out for you, following the handy step-by-step instructions with each activity.

You'll also need an inexpensive storage container for each activity. Sample labels for each container have been included at the back of this booklet (see pages 72-73). The best containers are those with clear sides and colourful, easy-to-put-on lids! Enlarge or reduce the labels to fit.

Then just add up to 30 enthusiastic children, some brief explanations from you and you're ready to go! I know you'll have as much fun using these games and activities in your classroom as I had creating them for you.

Copyright © Blake Education & Bev Dunbar

All rights reserved. The copyright holders authorise ONLY users of 'Number Games and Activities 0-10' to make photocopies of the photocopiable pages for their own or their students' immediate use within the teaching context. No other rights are granted without permission in writing from the publishers or under licence from the Copyright Licensing Agency Limited. Further details of such licences (for reprographic reproduction) may be obtained from the Copyright Licensing Agency Limited, of 90 Tottenham Court Road, London W1T 4LP.

First published by Blake Education, New South Wales, Australia

Published in 2002 by:
Nelson Thornes Ltd
Delta Place
27 Bath Rd
CHELTENHAM GL53 7TH
United Kingdom

02 03 04 05 06 / 10 9 8 7 6 5 4 3 2 1

A catalogue record for this book is available from the British Library.

ISBN 0-7487-6323-6

Series publisher: Katy Pike
Series editor: Garda Turner
Page layout and illustration: Janice Bowles
Additional illustrations p.23-27 from Mel Mann's "The Amazing Question and Answer Book", Playmore Inc Publishers and Waldman Publishing Corporation, New York NY, 1984.
Printed in Singapore, by Green Giant Press

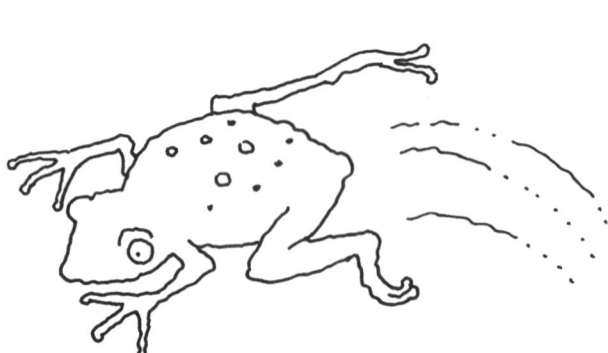

Contents

Catering for different abilities	2
Feed the Monkeys	4
Zebra Stripes	12
Balancing Balls	16
Find a Bone	21
How Hairy?	34
Set the Table	40
Something Fishy	46
Hopping Frogs	52
Freckles	58
Busy Bees	64
Storage Labels	72
Nets for Dice	74
Spinners	77

Catering for different abilities

Each game or activity can be adapted to suit the needs of at least three ability groups within your class. After introducing the materials (see the start of each teacher's page for ideas), allow time for free exploration, then explain one of the activities shown on the teacher's cards or from the summary below. The teacher's cards include a dot code to indicate the three levels. These cards can also be used by parent helpers in your classroom.

Level One

Counting and recognising numbers

- Working in groups of three or more, select one small numeral or number word card each and match the number of objects shown onto your large cards.

- Make up a story to match your actions.
  e.g. "This man had a fright. All his hair fell out except for these 6 hairs!"

Other group ideas

- Place objects onto a large card. Find the small card to match. Turn this face down, or cover it up. Ask a partner to guess the number on the small card.

- Place some objects onto a large card. Guess how many objects there are altogether. Check by counting, then find a small card to match.

- Use the 1-6 dot/numeral die or a 0-9 spinner. Race to collect the matching number of objects. Who has the most after each round?

- Use the 10-19 cards and the 10-19 spinner for extension groups. Children take a small card, a large card and find the matching number of objects.

Level Two

Ordering, comparing and estimating numbers

- In groups, pairs or individually, practise sorting the cards forwards/backwards into counting order.

- Find cards with the same/more/fewer objects than a given set.

- Make a pattern using the objects in your set. Ask a partner to predict the next few items in your pattern.

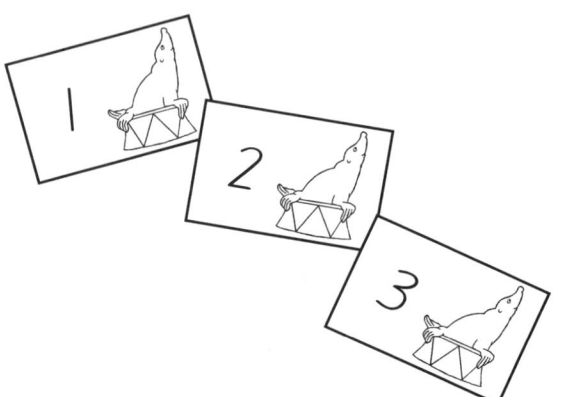

Other group ideas

◆ Mix up objects/counters between two or more sets. Invent an interesting pattern. Challenge a partner to identify then continue your pattern.

◆ For extension groups, place up to 19 objects onto a large card. Guess how many objects altogether. Check by counting. Put three or more cards from 0-19 into counting order forwards or backwards.

◆ Use the 7-12 die or the 10-19 spinner. Race to collect the matching number of objects. Who has the most after each round? The fewest? The same number?

Level Three

Addition and subtraction

◆ Identify how many objects you start with then add or take away objects to match a new number.

◆ Separate a given number of objects into two groups.

Other group ideas

◆ Identify whether there is an odd or an even number of objects. Explain how you know this.

◆ Make up a problem to match the theme.
e.g. "I'd like to have three more fish than you have. How many more fish do I need to put in my fish bowl?"

◆ Take a small card and match objects to a large card. Take another small card, match objects onto the same card. Guess how many altogether then check. Find a card to match this new number.

◆ Match objects to a card then challenge a partner to see how many equal groups they can make. e.g. "Can you make groups of three?"

◆ Use the 10-19 spinner. Collect the matching number of objects. Use the 0-9 spinner to identify how many to remove. Who has the most after each round? The fewest? The same number?

◆ Make up a game using the cards. e.g. Throw two dice, take that many objects. Try to be the first to get exactly 20 objects on your large card.

Feed the Monkeys

Introducing the activity

Discuss the way monkeys like to eat bananas. Pretend you are a zoo keeper. Each monkey likes to eat a specific number of bananas each day.

Outcomes

Compares and orders sets of objects using one-to-one correspondence.
Represents numerals using objects or drawings.
Counts collections up to nine.
Identifies more or less than a given number.
Demonstrates understanding of simple addition.
Counts on mentally to add small numbers.

How to make the game

♦ Make one copy of all the monkeys numbered 1 - 10 so that you have 10 monkeys. Colour each one, laminate and cut into individual monkeys.

♦ Make four copies of the bananas onto yellow paper (or copy and colour the bananas). Laminate and then cut out each banana.

♦ Copy, laminate and cut out the four activity cards.

♦ Place all the equipment into a storage container and label clearly. Use the label provided on page 72.

Extra materials needed

None

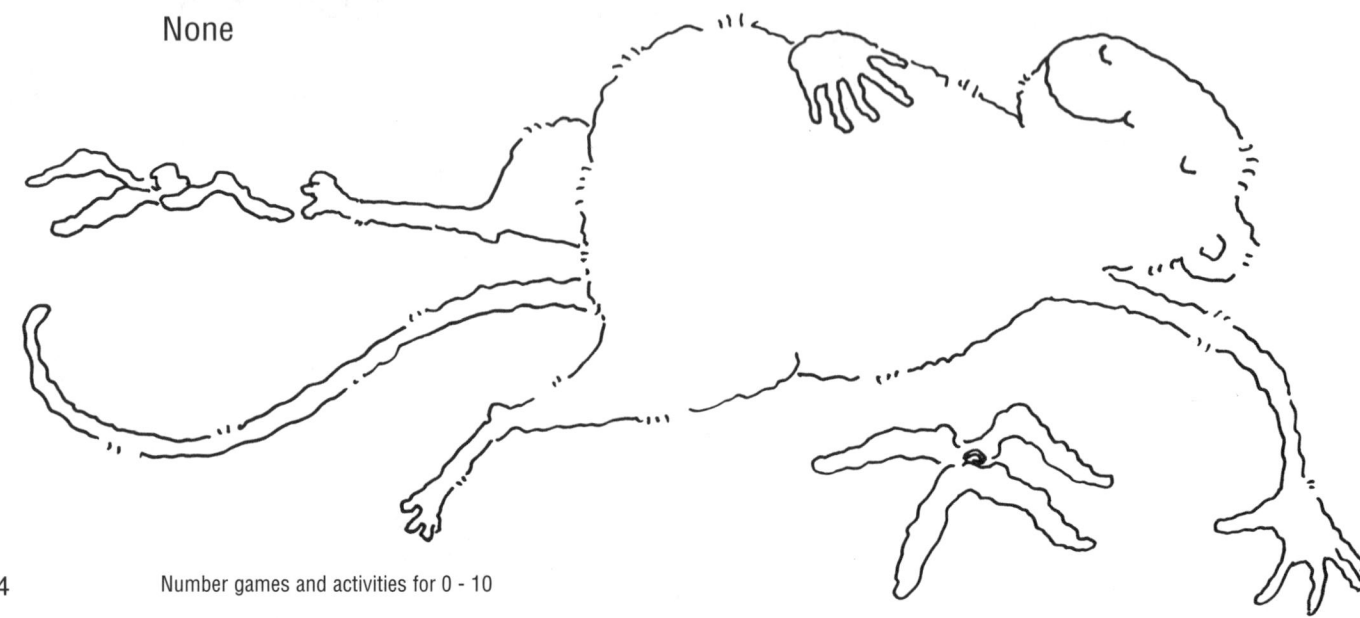

Feed a monkey

Pick a monkey. Look at the number. Feed the monkey the matching number of bananas.

How many bananas are small?

ONE or GROUP

•

Feed all the monkeys

Feed all the monkeys the matching number of bananas. Then turn each monkey over. Guess the monkey's number by looking at the bananas.

Can you put the monkeys into counting order?

GROUP

• •

Feed two monkeys

Take two monkeys. Match the bananas. How many bananas altogether? Guess first, then check.

ONE or PAIR

• • •

Bigger and smaller

Turn all the monkeys face down. Pick two monkeys. Which number is bigger?

Pick one monkey. What is the next number? What is the number before? How do you know?

PAIR

• • •

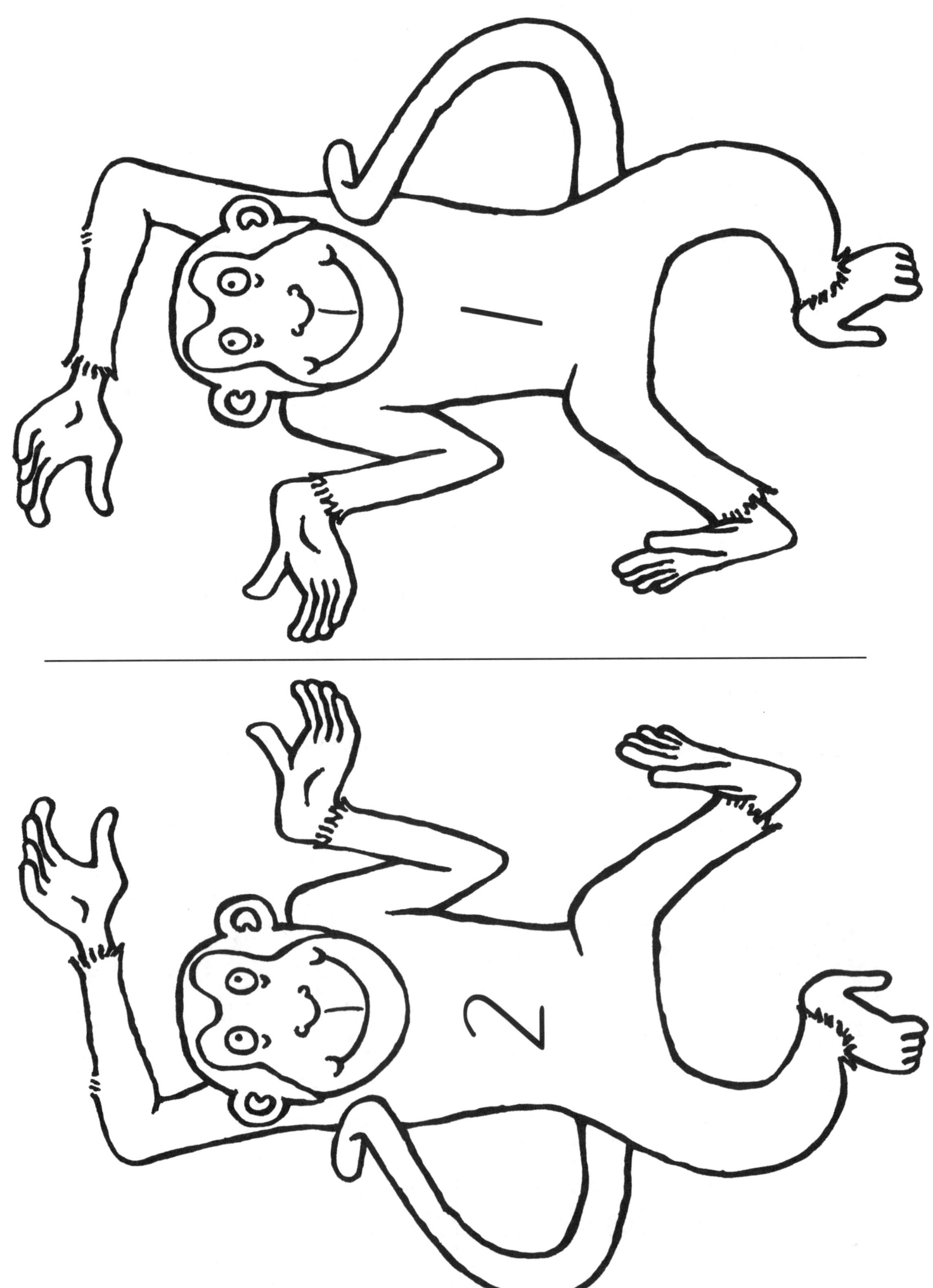

Number games and activities for 0 - 10

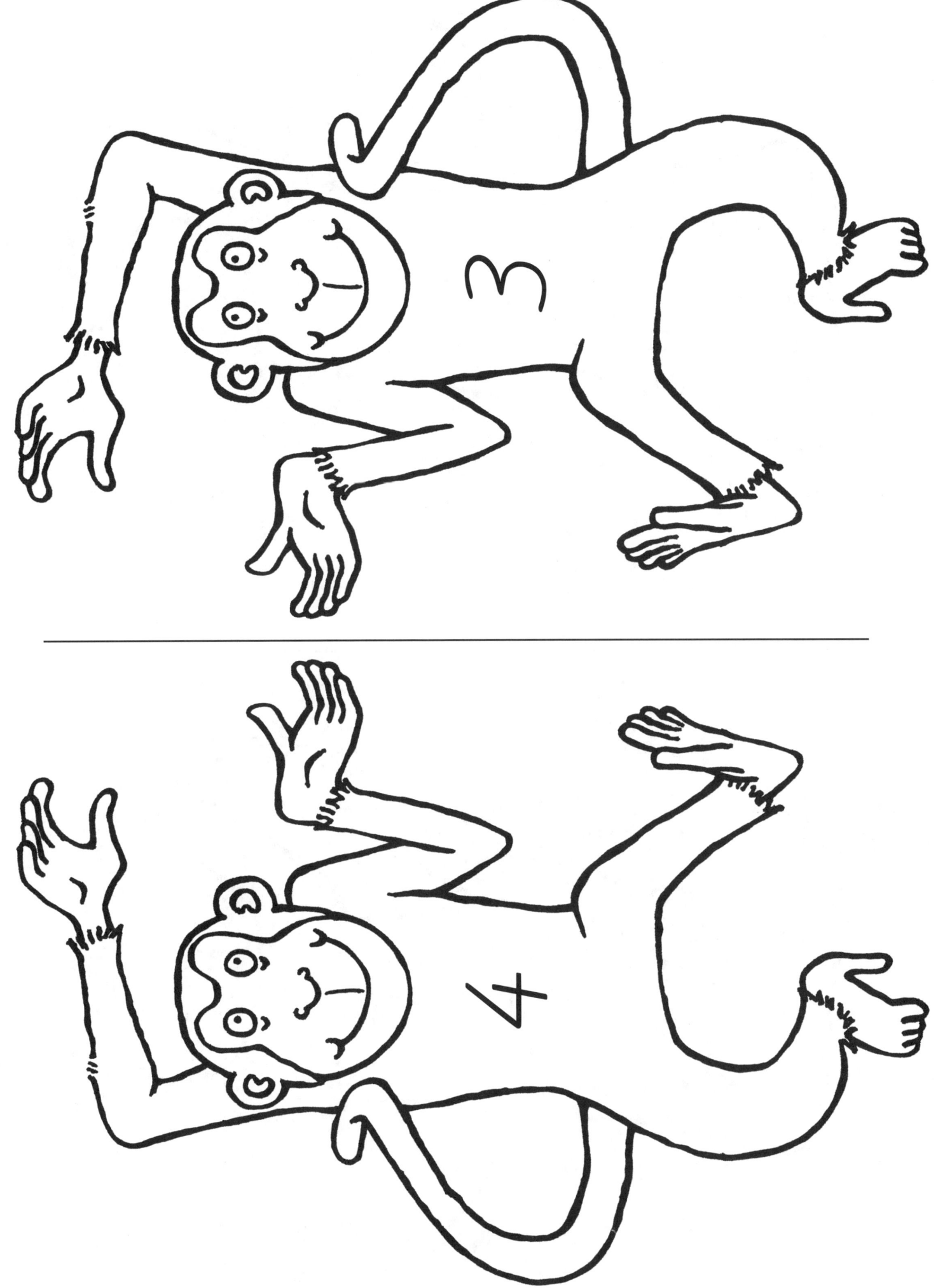

Number games and activities for 0 - 10

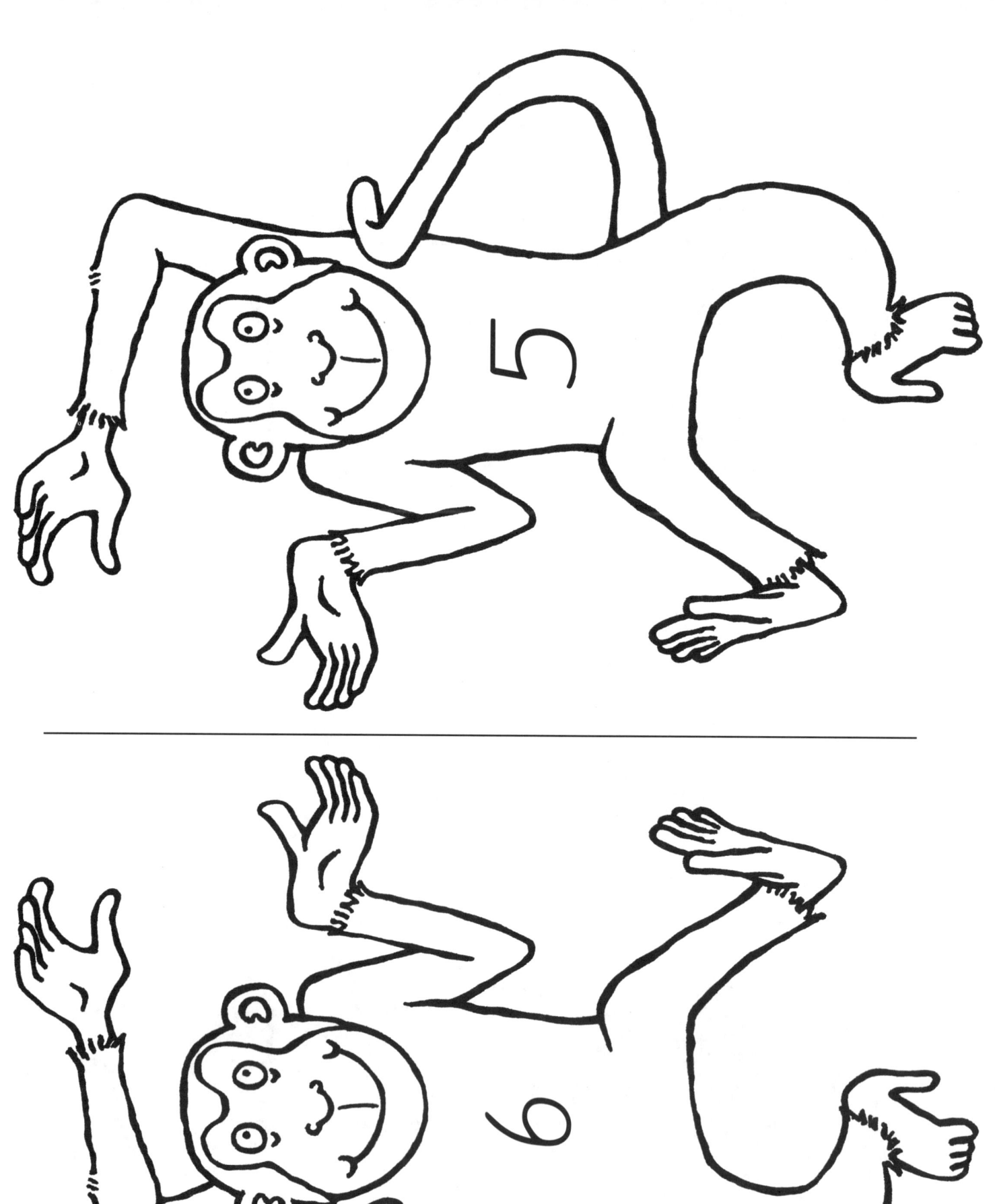

8   Number games and activities for 0 - 10

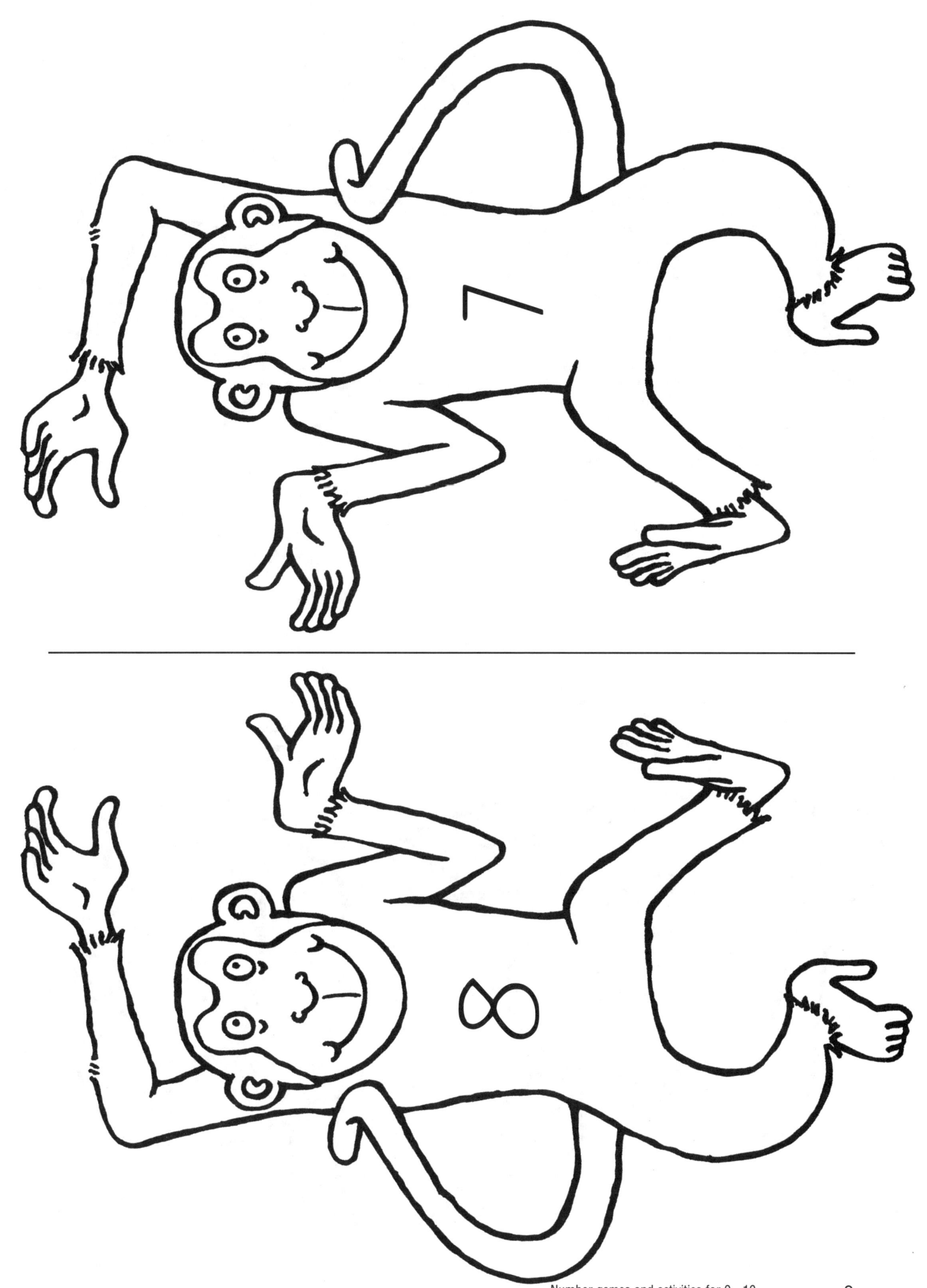

Number games and activities for 0 - 10

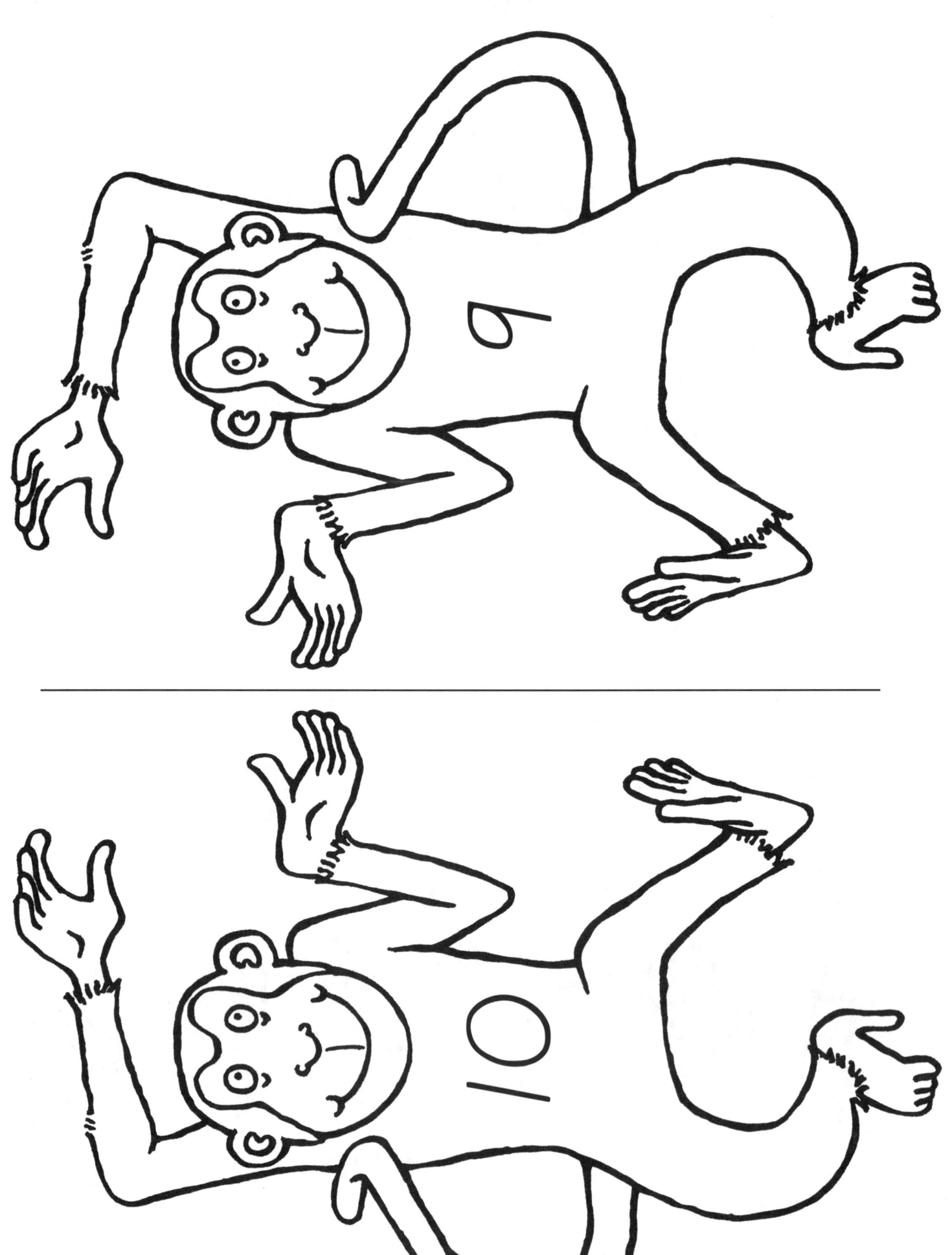

Bananas

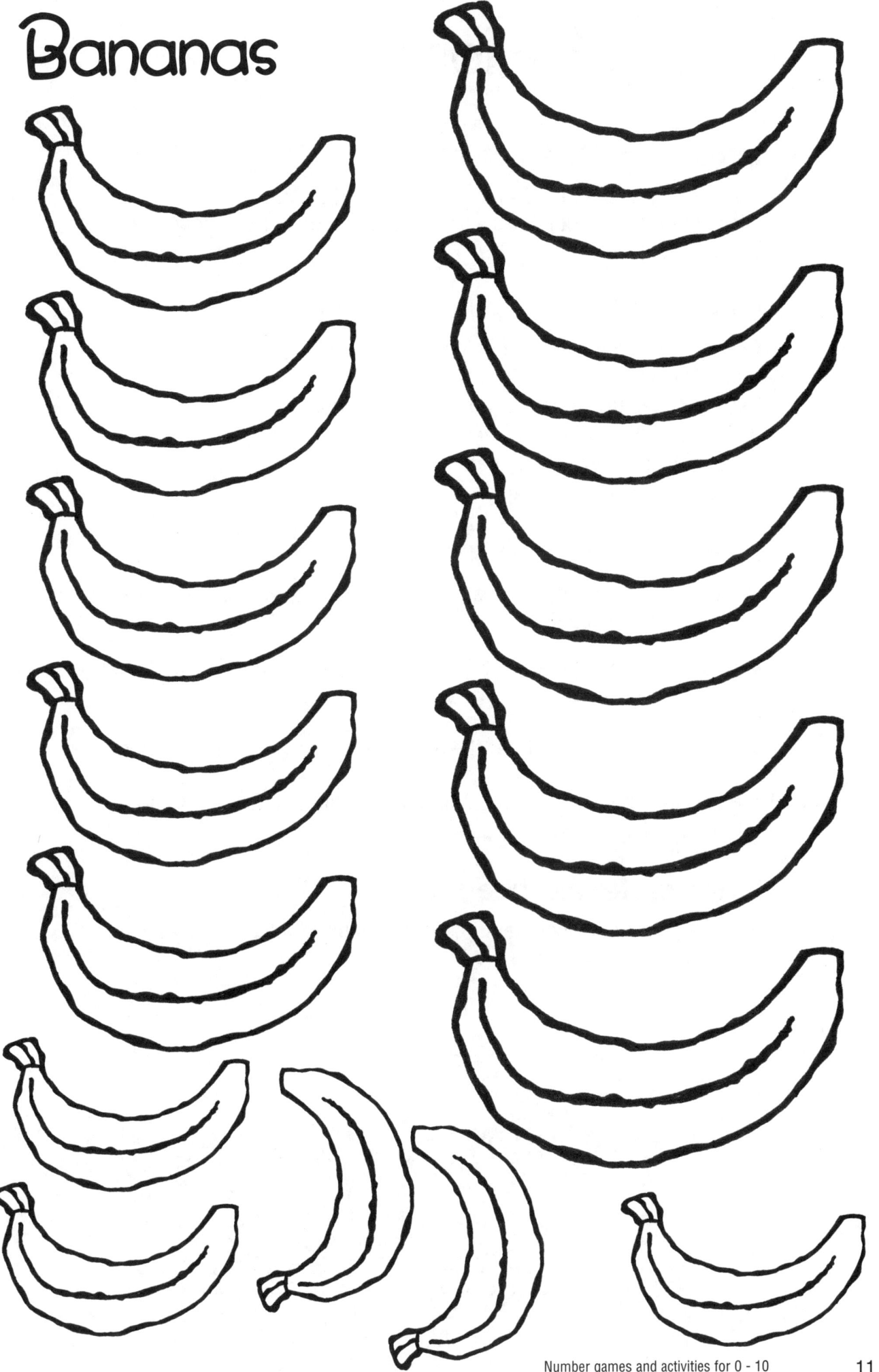

Zebra Stripes

Introducing the activity

Discuss how zebras have lots of stripes on their bodies. Pretend the stick counters are zebra stripes. The small cards tell you how many stripes you need.

Outcomes

Represents numerals using objects or drawings.
Counts collections up to nine.
Demonstrates understanding of simple addition.
Identifies and continues a given pattern.
Creates their own counting pattern.
Identifies more or less than a given number.

How to make the game

♦ Make ten A4 copies of the large zebra. You may like to add some decorative grass before laminating.

♦ Make one copy of the small 0 - 9 zebras. Colour, laminate and then cut out as small rectangular cards.

♦ Copy, laminate and cut out the four activity cards on the next page.

♦ Place all the equipment into a storage container and label clearly. Use the label provided on page 72.

Extra materials needed

45 - 50 plastic stick counters, including plenty of black ones as stripes for the zebra.

Zebra Stripes

Choose one large and one small zebra. Give your zebra the matching number of stripes.

Which zebra has the most stripes?
Which zebra has the fewest stripes?

GROUP

•

Coloured Stripes

Choose one large and one small zebra.
Use 2 colours for the stripes (eg 2 red and 3 yellow stripes for the 5 card.)
Count how many stripes in each colour.

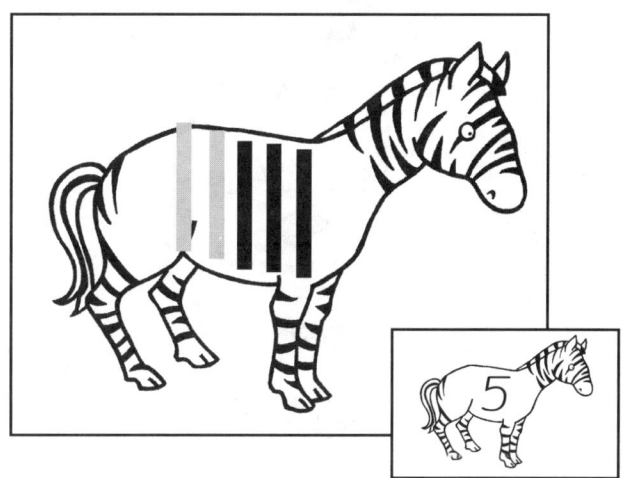

Record your discovery on paper.

 or
ONE   GROUP

• •

Zebra Stories

Tell your partner a zebra story.
Ask them to match the actions with their card and counters.
eg. One day the zebra woke up and had 4 yellow stripes. The next day there was one more stripe. How many altogether?

Find a small zebra card to match.

PAIR

• • •

Zebra Patterns

Make a pattern with the stripes
eg. black, yellow, black, yellow.
Ask your partner to say the next few colours and then continue the pattern. Swap roles.

PAIR

• • •

Number games and activities for 0 - 10

Balancing Balls

Introducing the activity

Discuss the way sea lions love to play together. A favourite trick when they are with humans is to balance balls on their noses. Imagine that you are playing ball with a friendly sea lion. The small balls tell you how many balls to use.

Outcomes

Represents numerals using objects or drawings.
Counts collections up to nine.
Demonstrates understanding of simple addition.
Counts on mentally to add small numbers.
Demonstrates understanding of simple fractions as 'equal shares'.

How to make the game

- ♦ Make ten A4 copies of the large sea lion card. Colour these in with crayons, then laminate.

- ♦ Make three copies of the balls page. Colour brightly, laminate and cut out as individual balls.

- ♦ Make one copy of the small sea lions 0 - 9 page. Laminate and cut out as small rectangular cards.

- ♦ Copy, laminate and cut out the four activity cards on the next page.

- ♦ Place all the equipment into a storage container and label clearly. Use the label provided on page 72.

Extra materials needed

None

Balancing Balls

Select one small sea lion and one large sea lion card.
Balance the matching number of balls on the sea lion's nose.

Hide the card. Ask your partner to guess the number.

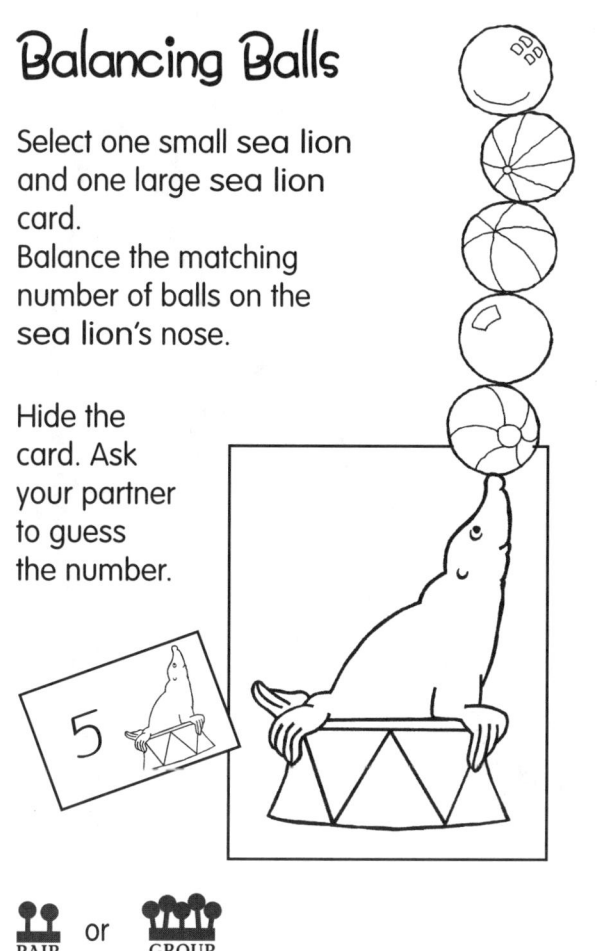

PAIR or GROUP •

Two sea lions

Take a handful of balls and 2 large sea lions.
Share the balls between the 2 sea lions.
Is there a fair share? Why?

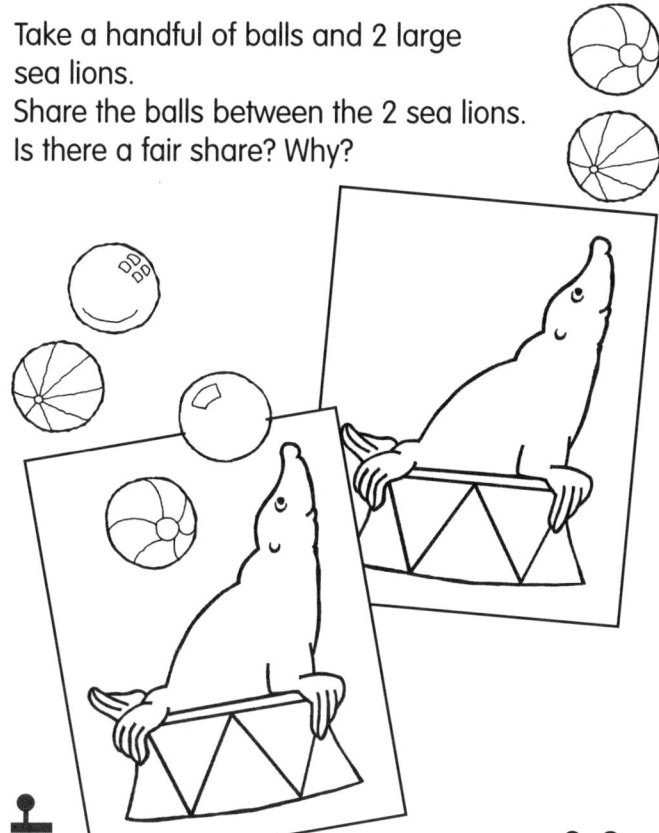

ONE • •

Pattern balls

Make a pattern with your balls, eg red, blue, red, blue.
Ask your partner to continue the pattern.
Swap roles.

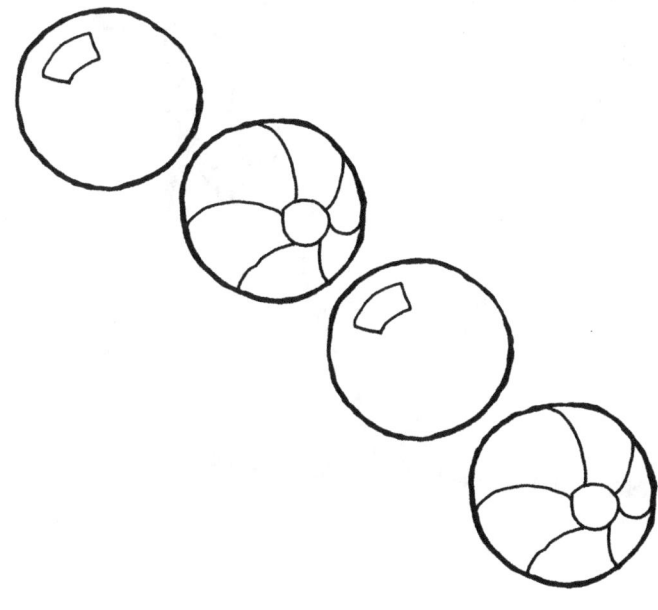

PAIR or GROUP • •

Secret number

Work with a partner.
Put a secret number of balls on your sea lion's nose. Reveal both sea lions.
Do you have the same number?
Do you have more or fewer balls than your partner?
Guess, then check.

PAIR • • •

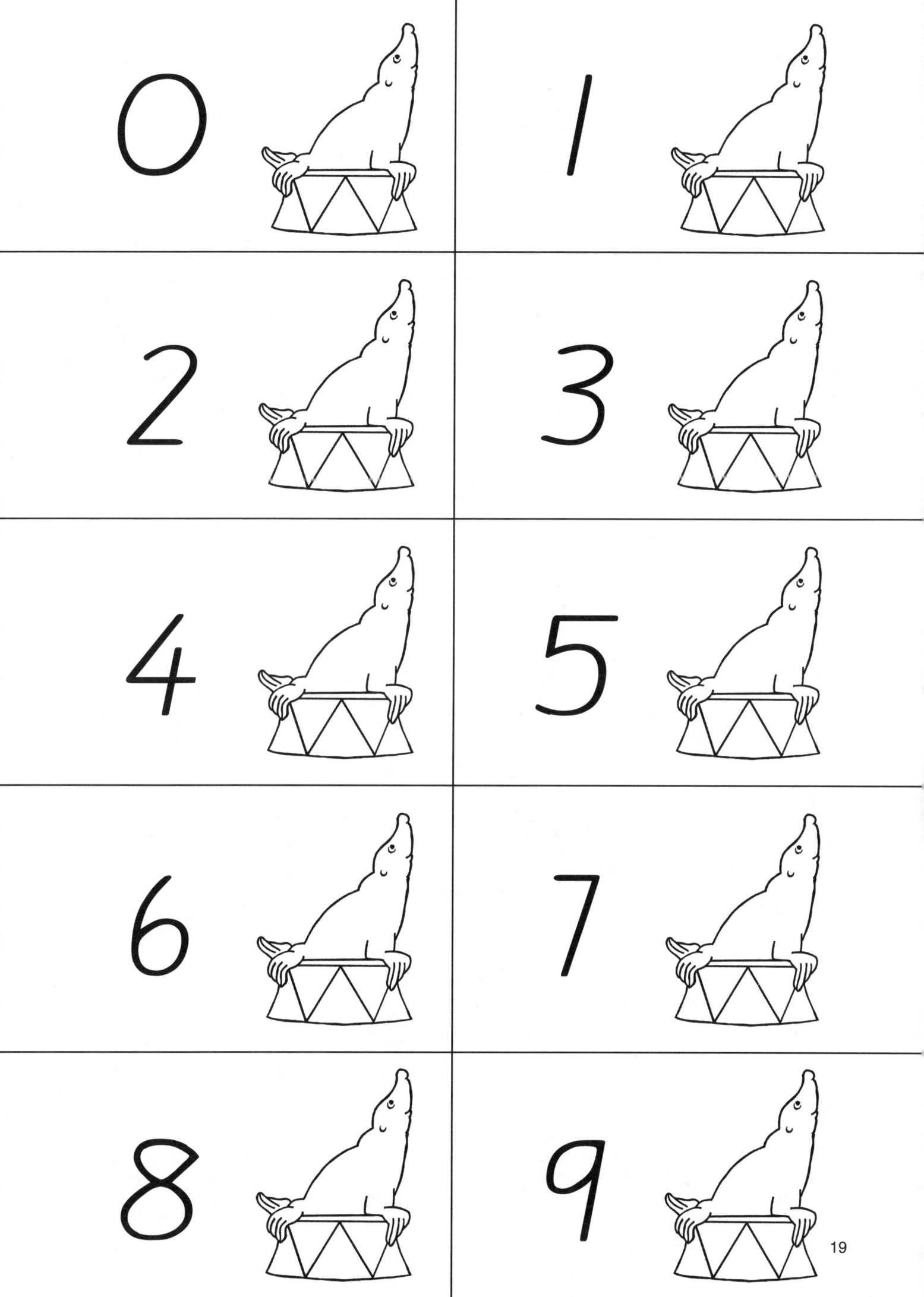

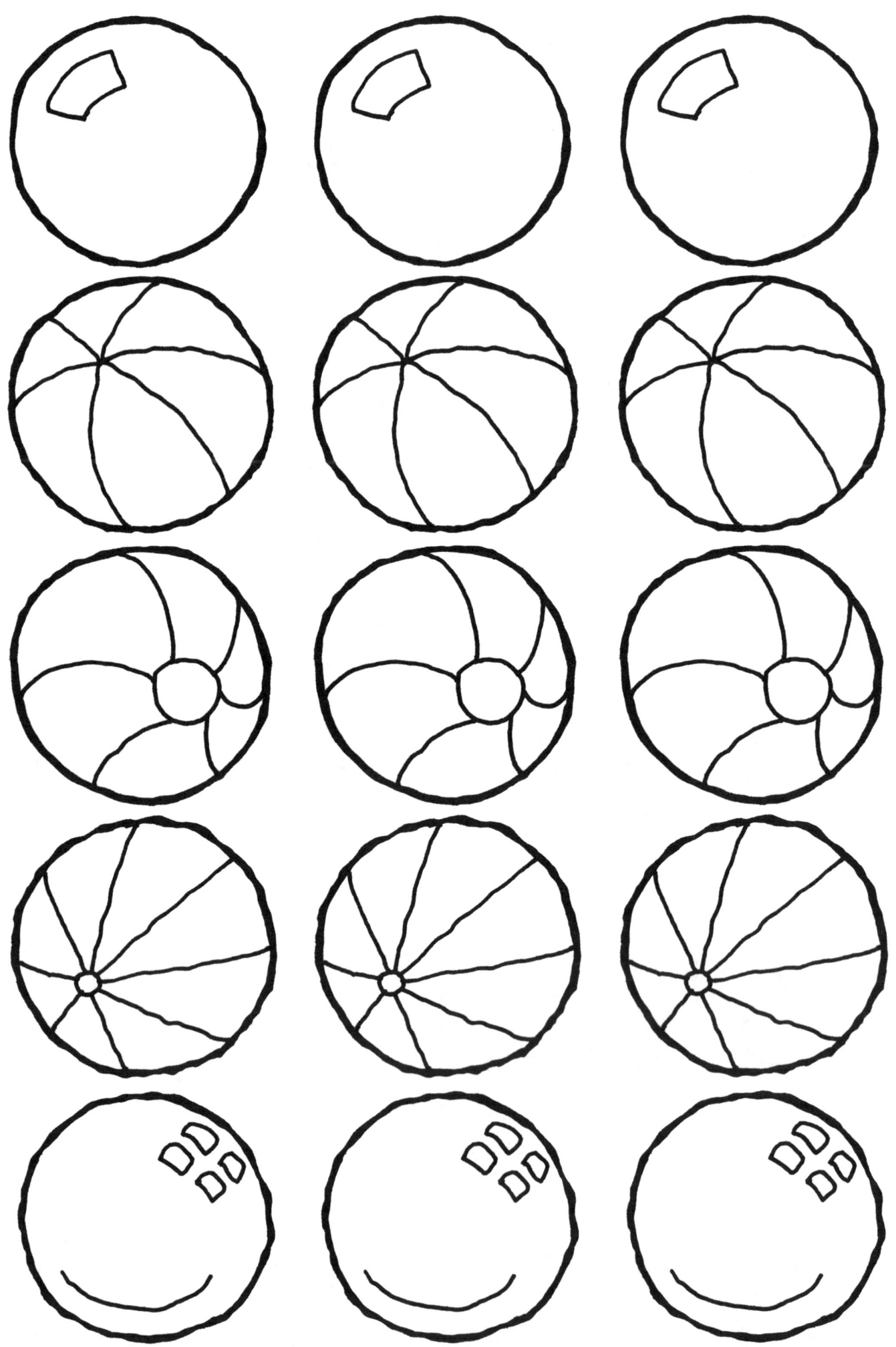

Find a Bone

Introducing the activity

Discuss dogs in general and any antics they get up to as pets. Discuss the characters of the dogs here. Each one likes to collect a certain number of bones.

Outcomes

Rote counts forwards to ...
Represents numerals using objects or drawings.
Counts collections up to ten.
Represents numbers in symbols and words.
Places objects into order by size, shape or number.
Identifies missing numbers in a given counting pattern.
Demonstrates understanding of simple fractions as 'equal shares'.

How to make the game

♦ Make one copy of each of the dog pages, so that you have ten dogs in all. Colour each dog, laminate and cut into ten A5 rectangular cards.

♦ Make one copy of each dog bone page - symbol, numeral and number words. Colour in, laminate and cut out as individual bones.

♦ Copy, laminate and cut out the four activity cards on the next page.

♦ Place all the equipment into a storage container and label clearly. Use the label provided on page 72.

Extra materials needed

None

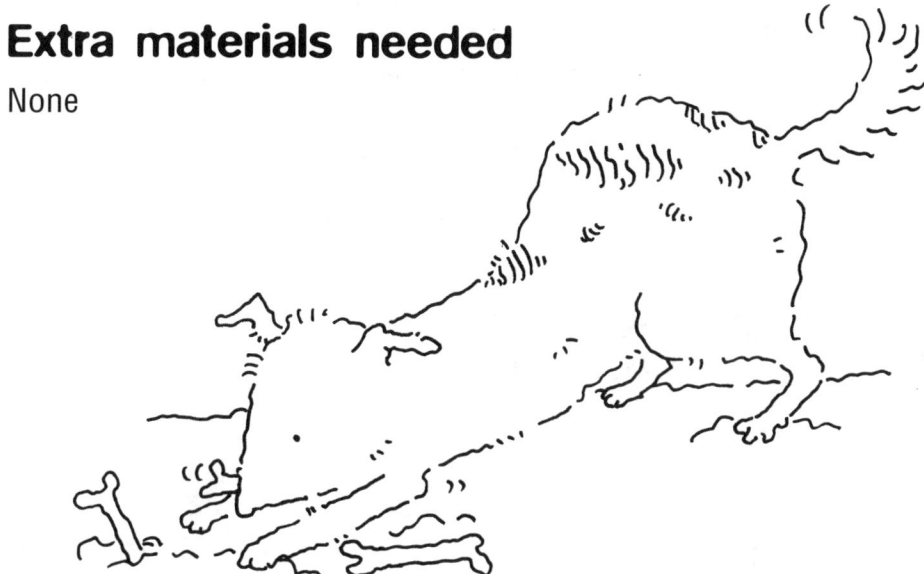

Number games and activities for 0 - 10

Find three Bones

Take a large dog card. Find a matching set of symbols/numeral/number word bones. Compare them with a partner's bones.

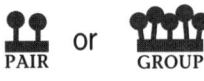 or •
PAIR   GROUP

Sort the Bones

Sort the bones into three piles - symbols, numerals and number words. Sort each group into counting order.

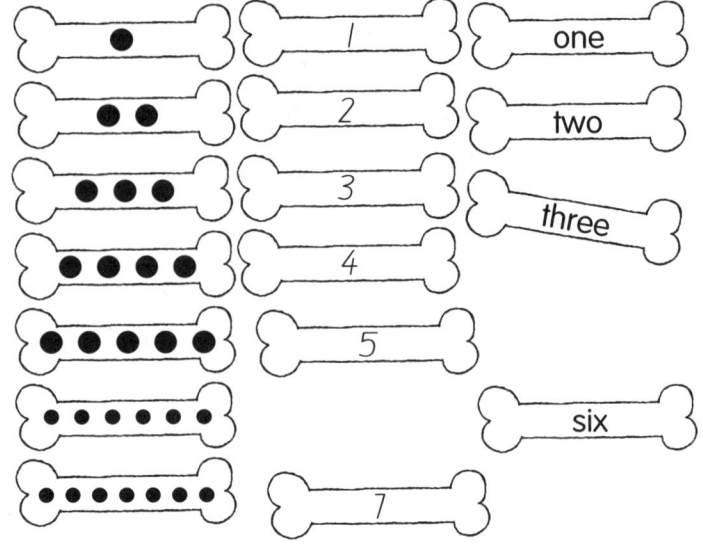

Can you sort them backwards too?

 or   ••
ONE PAIR   GROUP

Guess the Number

Work with a partner. Hold up a symbol bone. Ask your partner to guess how many 'dots'. Swap roles.

Hold up a numeral bone. Ask your partner to tell you the number that comes before or after. Swap roles.

PAIR   •••

Share the bones

Take 3 dogs each and a handful of bones. Can you share your bones equally between your 3 dogs? Guess first, then check.
Find 2 ways to sort the bones so that it is not a fair share.

PAIR   •••

Number games and activities for 0 - 10   23

Number games and activities for 0 - 10

Number games and activities for 0 - 10

26 Number games and activities for 0 - 10

Number games and activities for 0 - 10

Number games and activities for 0 - 10

Number games and activities for 0 - 10

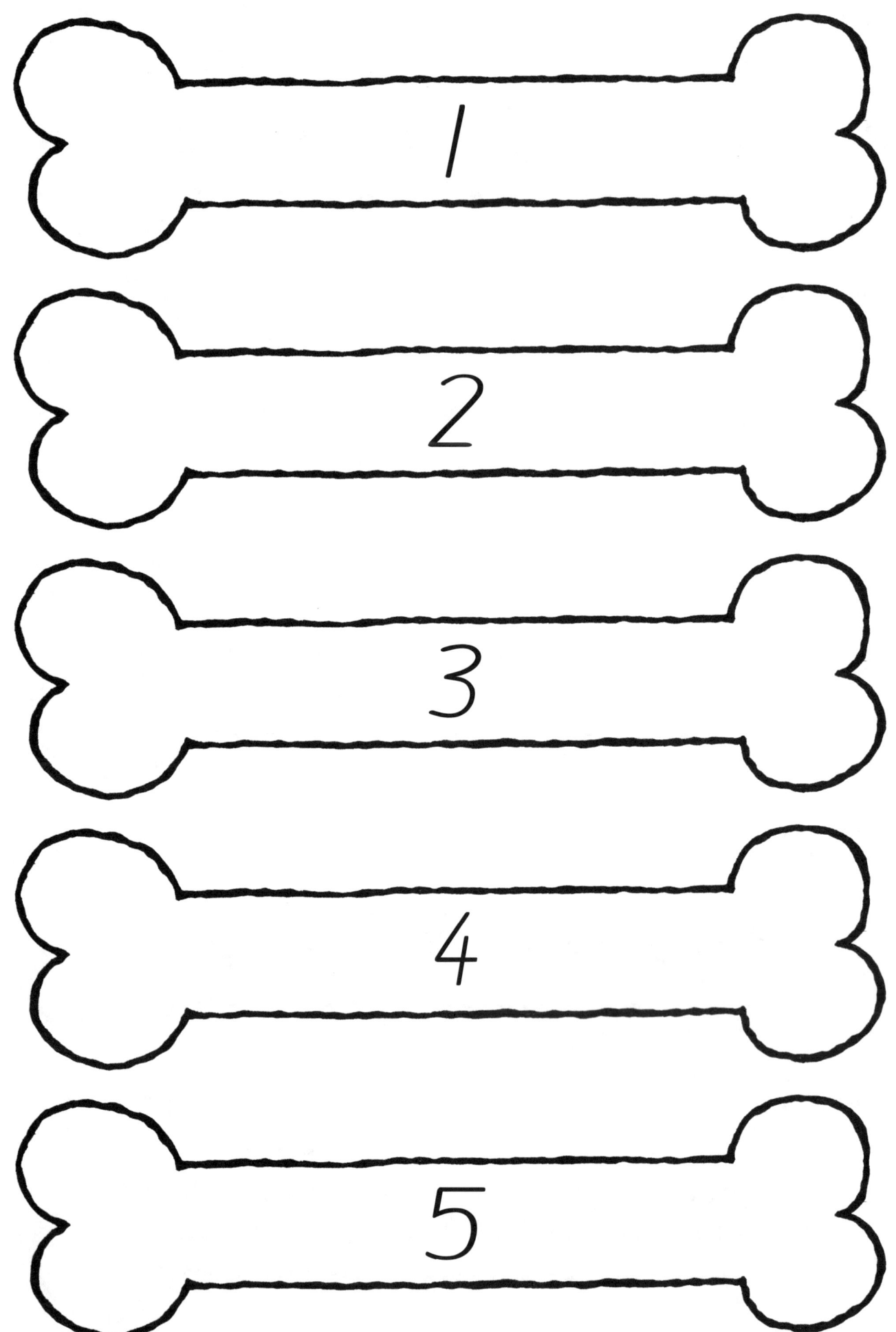

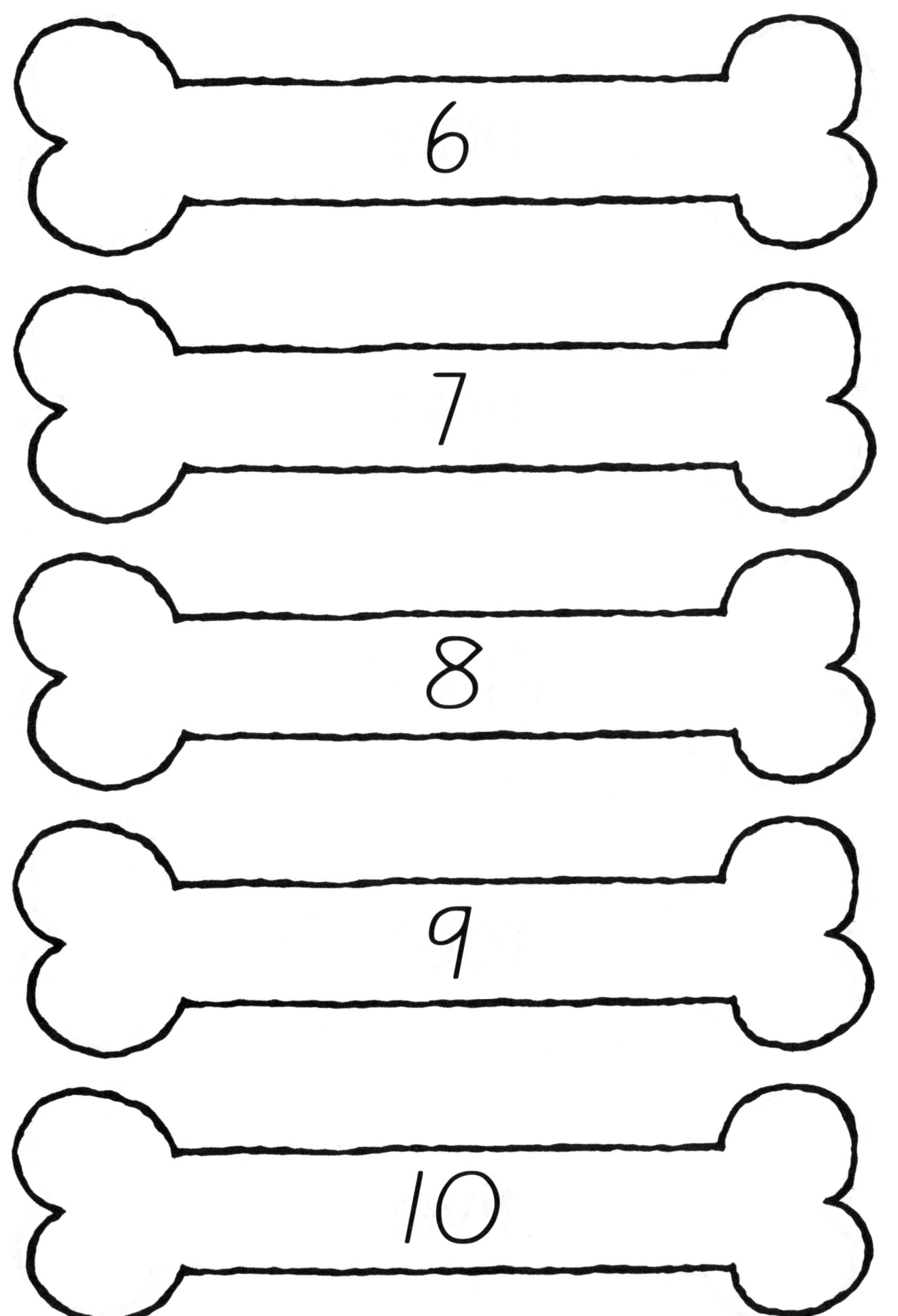

Number games and activities for 0 - 10

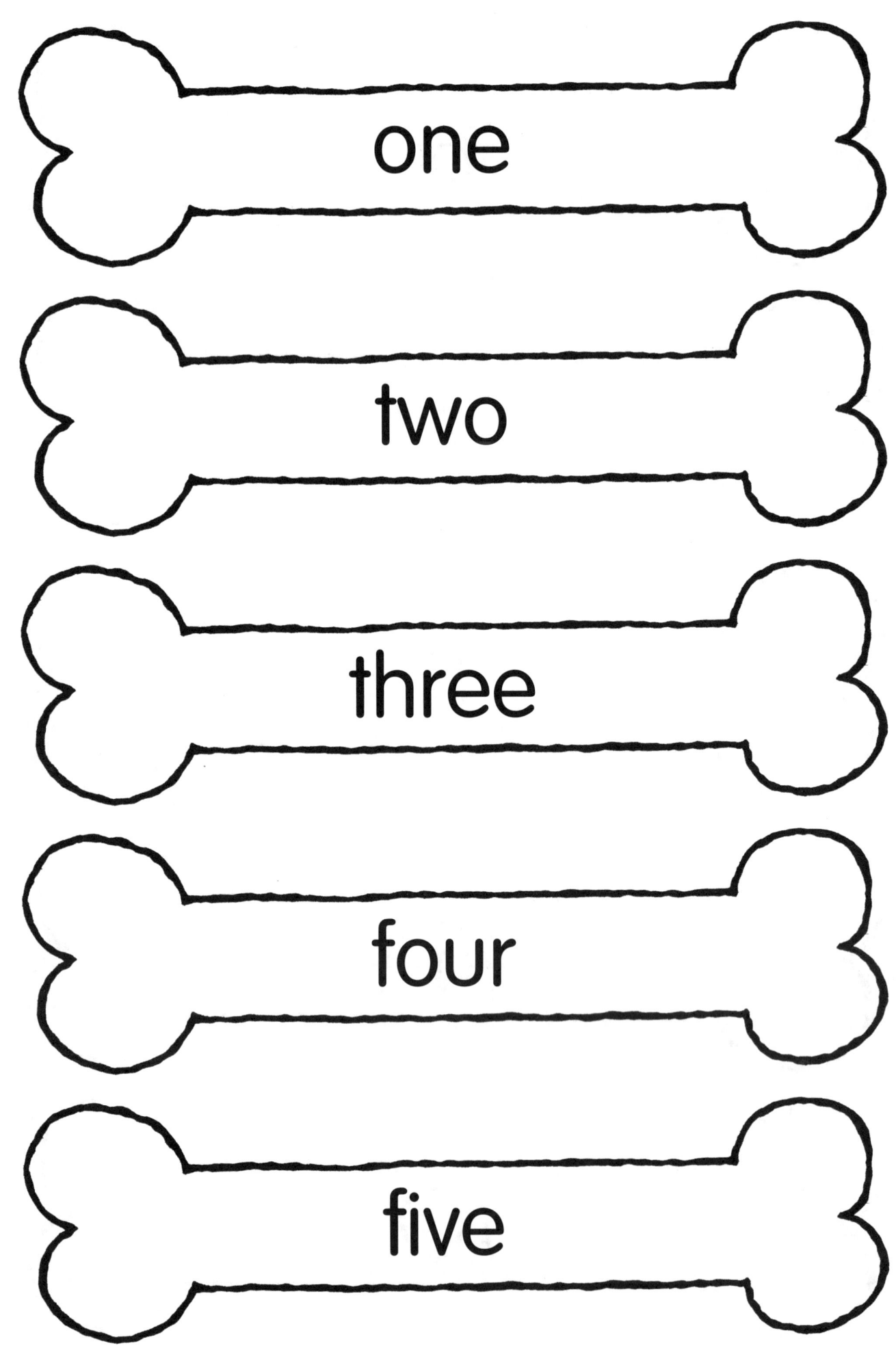

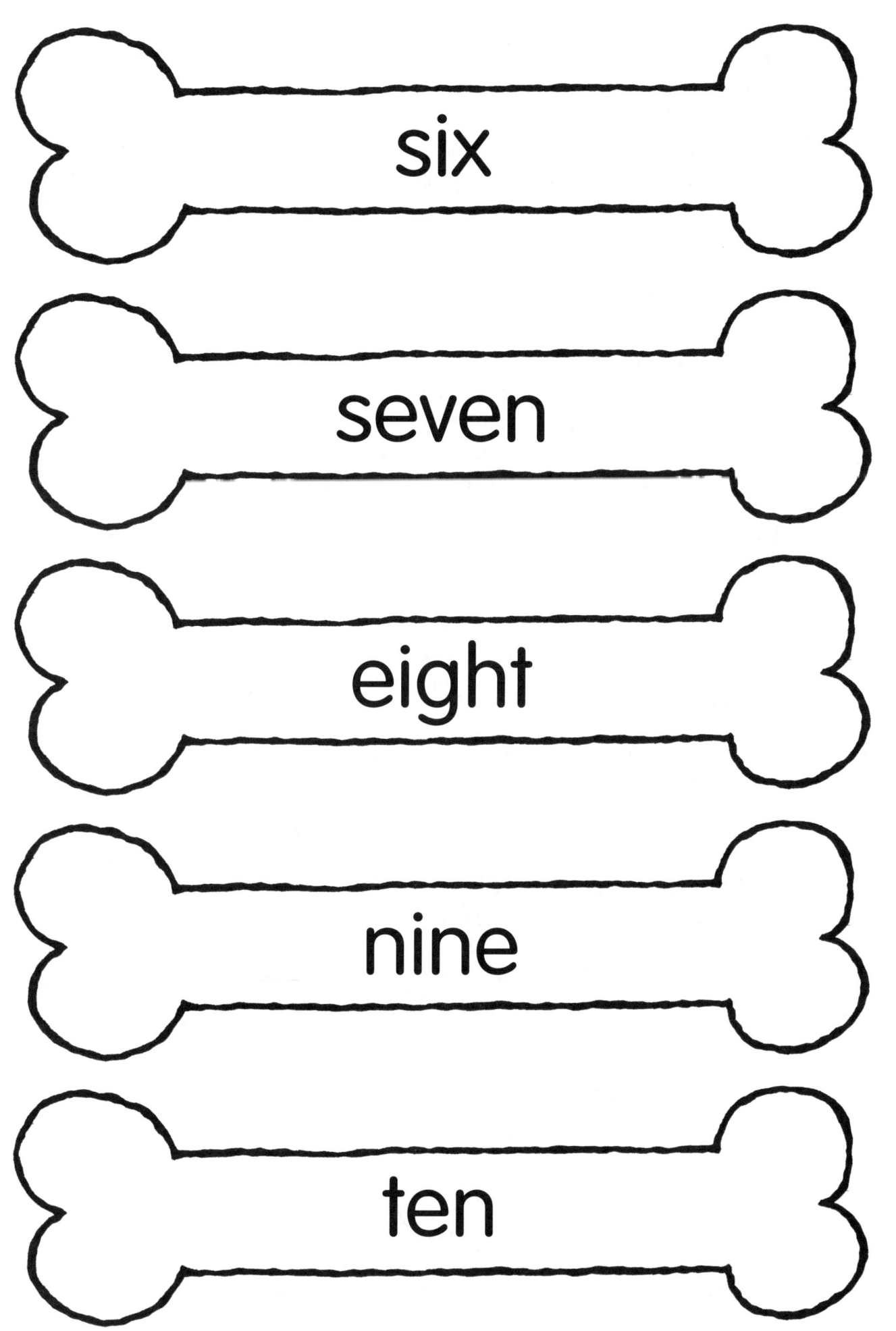

How Hairy?

Introducing the activity

Discuss how Mr Hairy is now bald. He loves to imagine what it would be like to have hair. Pretend each lollipop stick is a strand of hair on his head.

Outcomes

Represents numerals using objects or drawings.
Counts collections up to ten.
Places objects into order by size, shape or number.
Invents and records number stories.
Demonstrates conservation of number with up to 10 objects.
Understands simple subtraction and records results.

How to make the game

♦ Make ten A4 copies of the large 'Hairy' card. Colour these in with crayons, then laminate.

♦ Make one copy of the 'Hairy' 0 - 9 page. Make one copy of the 'Hairy' zero to nine page too. Laminate and cut out as small rectangular cards.

♦ For extension activities, copy the 10 - 19 'Hairy' cards. Laminate and cut out. You will need extra lollipop sticks too.

♦ Copy, laminate and cut out the four activity cards on the next page.

♦ Place all the equipment into a storage container and label clearly. Use the label provided on page 72.

Extra materials needed

45 - 50 coloured lollipop sticks.

How Hairy?

Select one small card and one 'Mr Hairy' card. Place the matching number of lollipop sticks on Mr Hairy's head. Find different ways to arrange his hair.

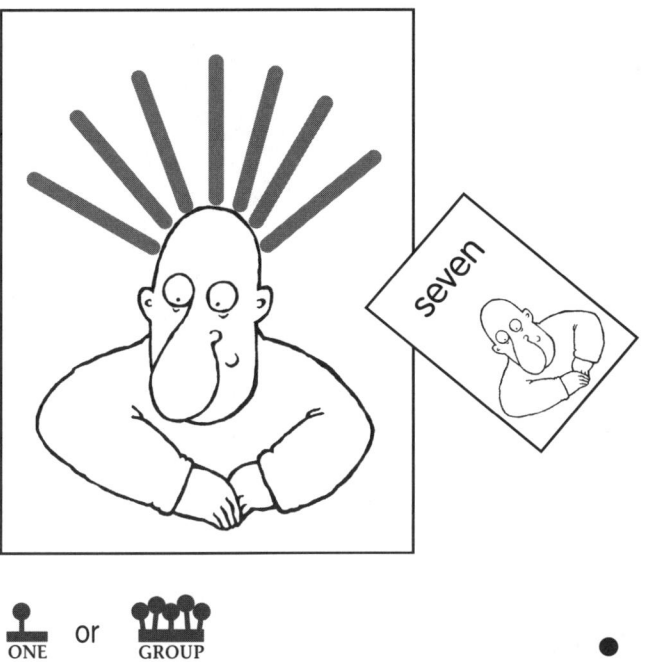

ONE or GROUP

The Hairiest

Put hair on 5 Mr Hairy cards. Ask your partner to put them in order from the least to the most hair. Find the small number card to match too!

PAIR

Hairy stories

Work with a partner. Tell each other stories about Mr Hairy. Model each story with lollipop sticks.
eg. Mr Hairy has 10 strands of hair. After scratching his head 3 strands fall out. How many strands are there now?

PAIR   Record one of your stories.

A handful of hair

Take a handful of sticks. Guess how many you have. Count them. Place them on a Mr Hairy card. Find a number word card to match. Ask your partner to rearrange Mr Hairy's hair. Guess how many strands now? Count the sticks again. Did moving the sticks change the number? Why?

PAIR

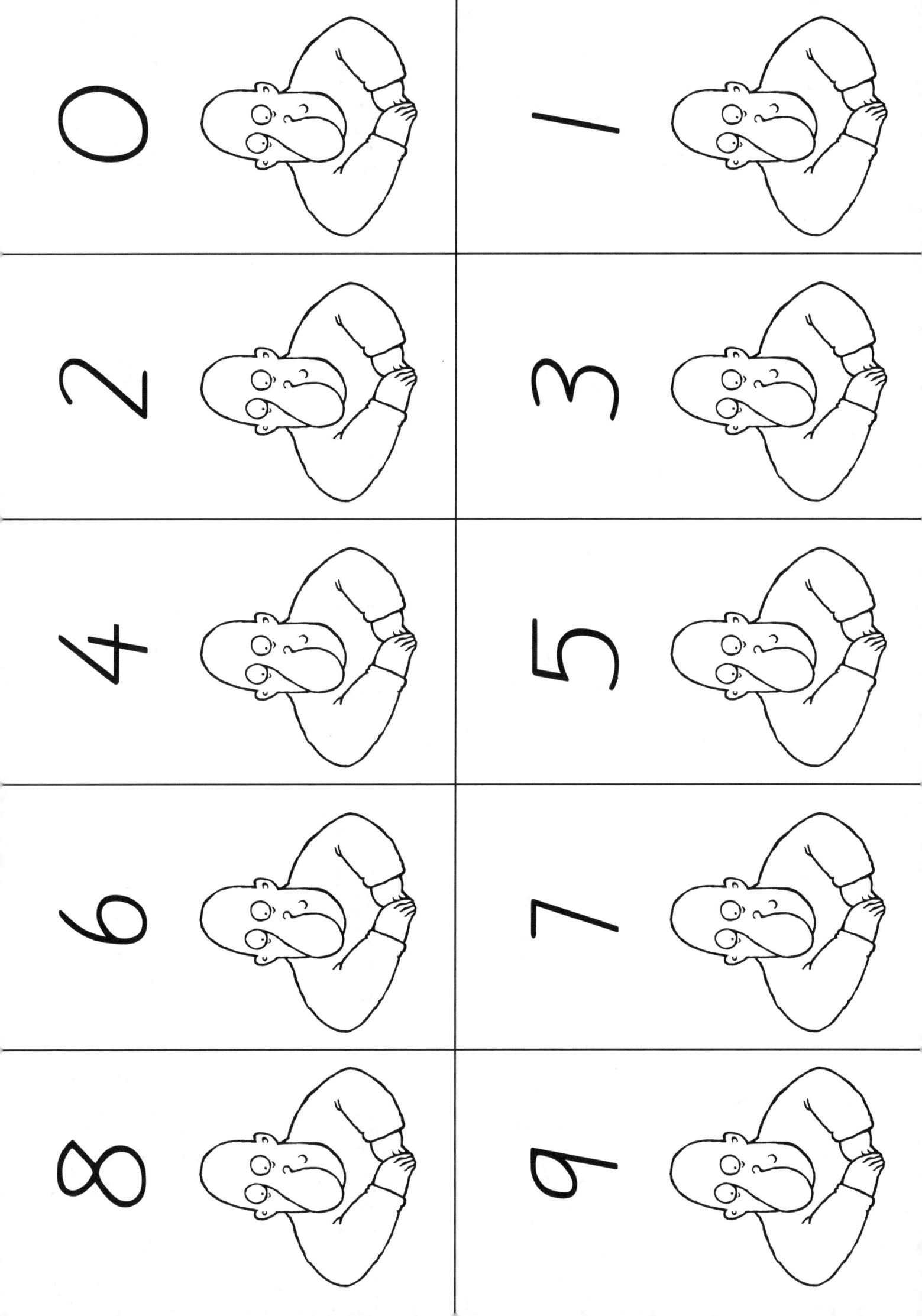

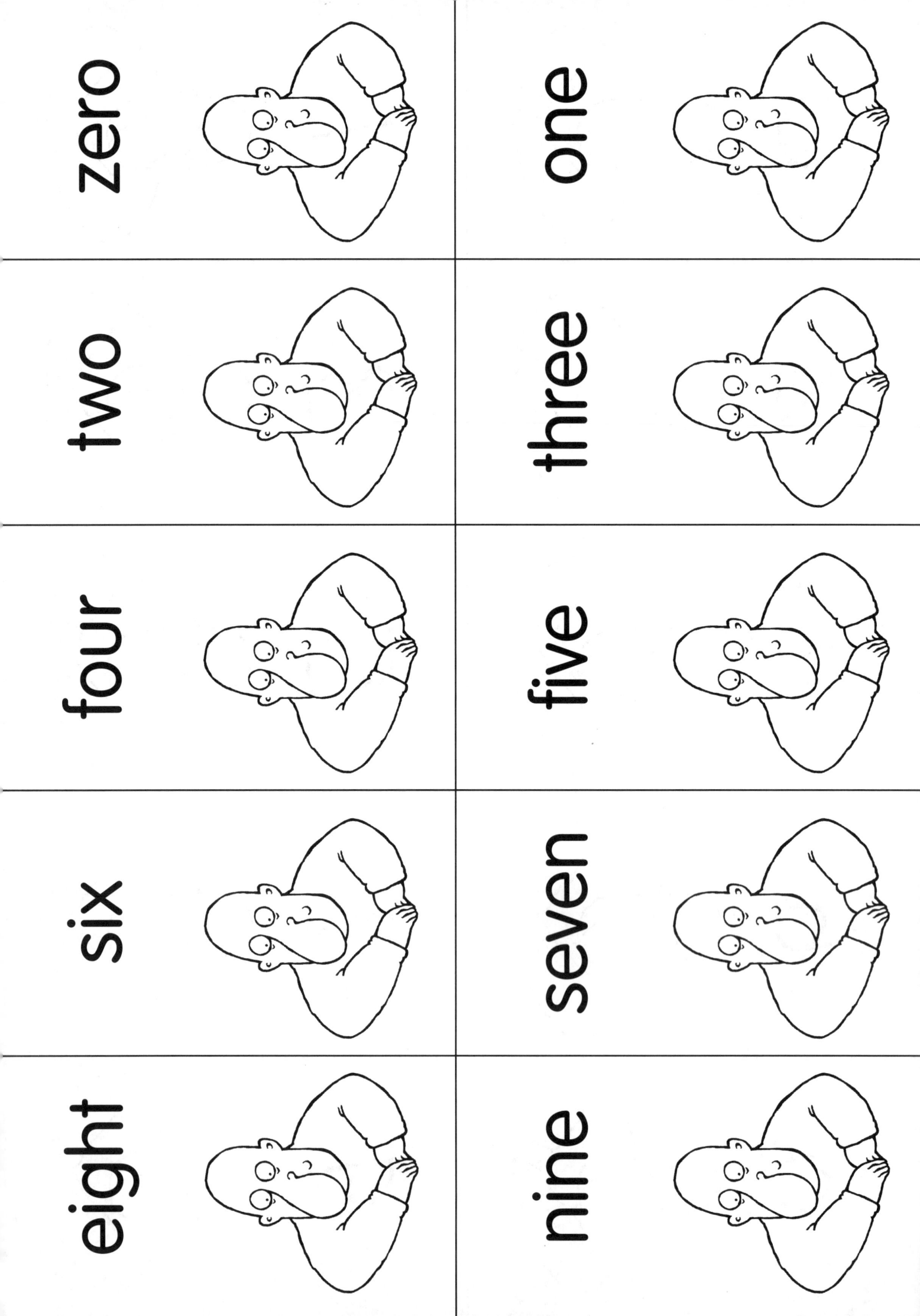

10	11
12	13
14	15
16	17
18	19

Set the Table

Introducing the activity

Discuss how we set the table with a knife, fork, spoon and plate for each person. Discuss where you put each item. The small cards tell you how many doughnuts to put on each plate. You can then find the knife, fork and spoon to match.

Outcomes

Compares and orders sets of objects using one-to-one correspondence.
Represents numerals using objects or drawings.
Counts collections up to ten.
Represents numbers in symbols and words.
Identifies a group of objects as odd or even.
Places objects into order by size, shape or number.
Identifies missing numbers in a given counting pattern.

How to make the game

♦ On each fork, write a numeral from 0 - 9. On each knife write the number words from zero to nine. On each spoon draw some symbols in sets from 0 to 9.

♦ Make 3 copies of the doughnuts page to make 48 doughnuts in all. Colour each doughnut, then laminate. Cut out as individual doughnuts.

♦ Make one copy of the 0 - 9 doughnuts. These are the activity cards that indicate how many doughnuts to put on each paper plate. Laminate and cut into small rectangular cards.

♦ For extension activities, copy the 10 - 19 doughnut cards. Laminate and cut out. You will need plenty more copies of the doughnut page.

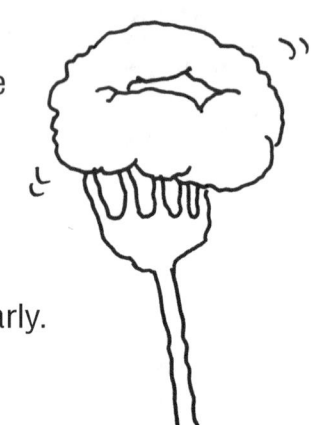

♦ Copy, laminate and cut out the four activity cards on the next page.

♦ Place all the equipment into a storage container and label clearly. Use the label provided on page 73.

Extra materials needed

A colourful set of 10 plastic knives, forks and spoons.
10 colourful paper plates.

Number games and activities for 0 - 10

Set the Table

Select a small card. Place the matching number of doughnuts onto a plate. Find the matching knife, fork and spoon.

PAIR or GROUP •

Missing Numbers

Sort the knives into counting order, then all the forks, then all the spoons.
Hide some. Ask your partner to tell you the missing numbers. Swap roles.

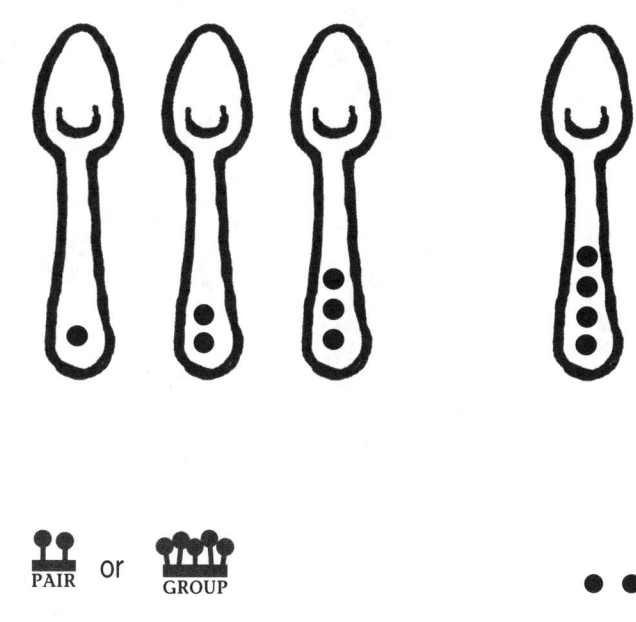

PAIR or GROUP ••

How many doughnuts?

Work with a partner. Arrange a secret number of doughnuts on your plate.
Show them to each other for about 2 seconds then hide them again.
Guess whether you both have the same, more or fewer doughnuts than each other.
Check by matching them one for one.
Find a small card to match your number of doughnuts.

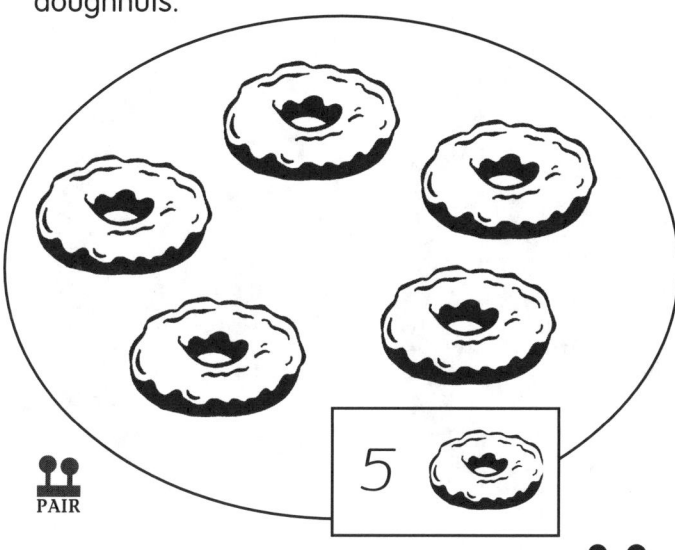

PAIR ••

Odd or Even

Select a small card.
Place the matching number of doughnuts onto a plate. Do you have an odd or even number of doughnuts? How do you know?

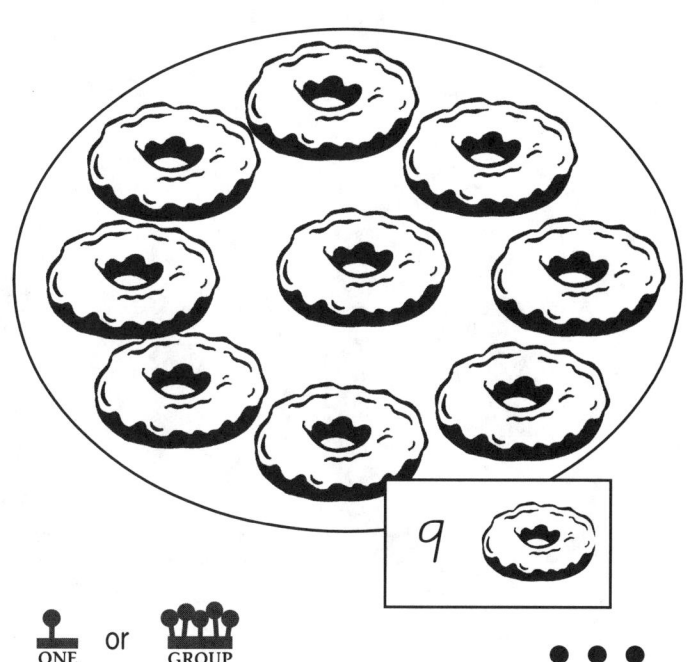

ONE or GROUP •••

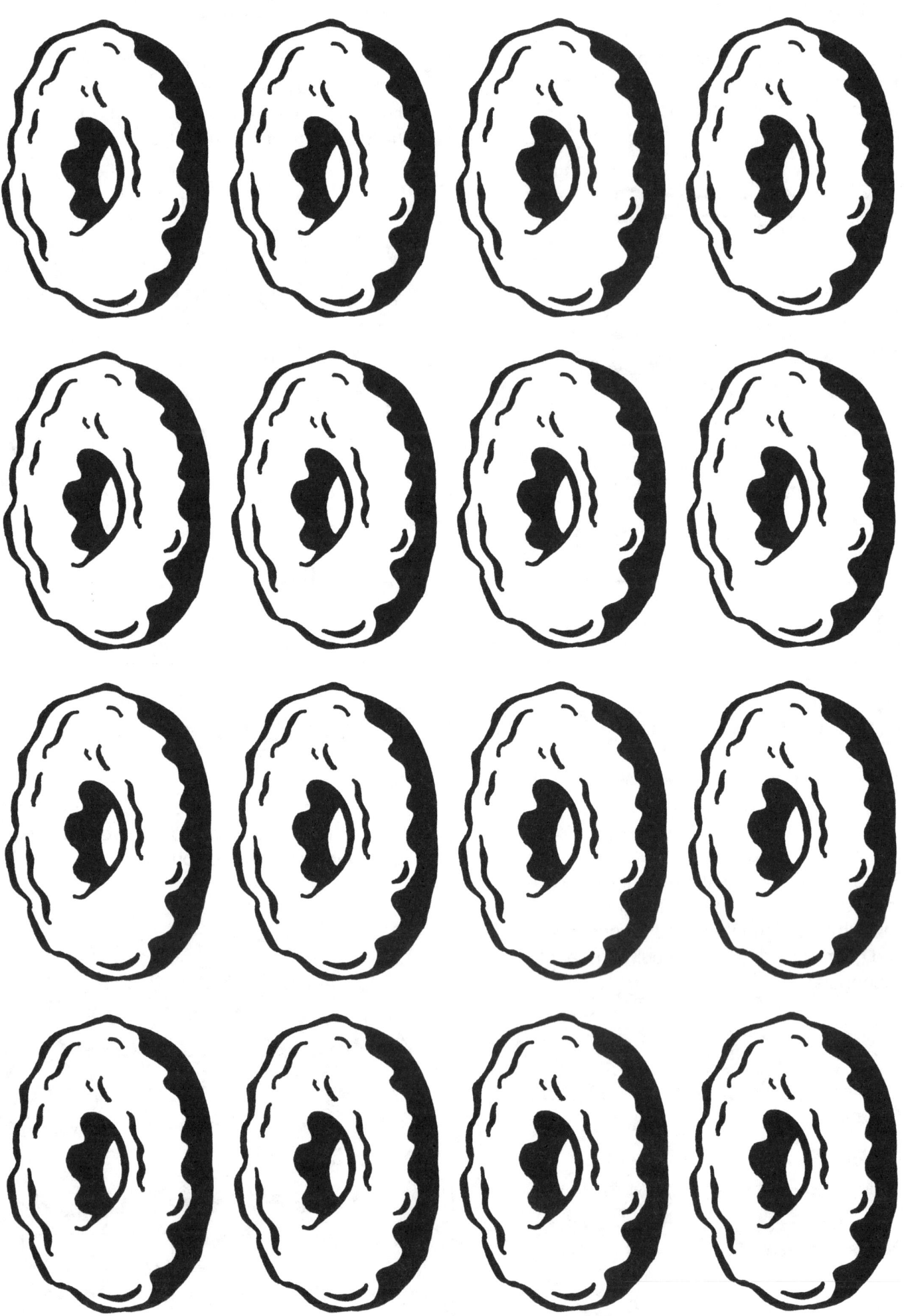

0  1

2  3

4  5

6  7

8  9

zero 	one 
two 	three 
four 	five 
six 	seven 
eight 	nine 

10 	11 
12 	13 
14 	15 
16 	17 
18 	19 

Something Fishy

Introducing the activity

Pretend the fish are swimming around in each fishbowl. The small cards show you how many fish go in each bowl.

Outcomes

Sorts and classifies objects into two or more sets.
Explains the sorting criterion for a given set.
Identifies similarities and differences in objects and sets.
Places objects into order by size, shape or number.
Rote counts forwards to ...
Represents numerals using objects or drawings.
Counts collections up to ten.
Identifies and continues a given pattern.
Records patterns by writing or drawing.
Creates their own counting patterns.
Demonstrates understanding of simple addition and subtraction.

How to make the game

♦ Make ten A4 copies of the large fishbowl. Colour each bowl, then laminate.

♦ Make three copies of the fish page to make 60 fish altogether. Colour in, laminate and cut out as individual fish.

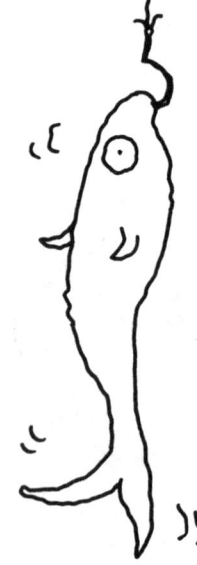

♦ Copy the small 0 - 9 fishbowl page. These are the activity cards which indicate how many fish to place in each large fishbowl.

♦ For extension activities, copy the 10 - 19 fishbowls as well. Laminate and cut out. You will also need more copies of the fish.

♦ Copy, laminate and cut out the four activity cards on the next page.

♦ Place all the equipment into a storage container and label clearly. Use the label provided on page 73.

Extra materials needed

0-9 or 10-19 spinner.

How Many Fish?

Take a large fishbowl each and a small card. Put the matching number of fish into your fishbowl. Turn over another card each. Add or remove some fish to match the new card.

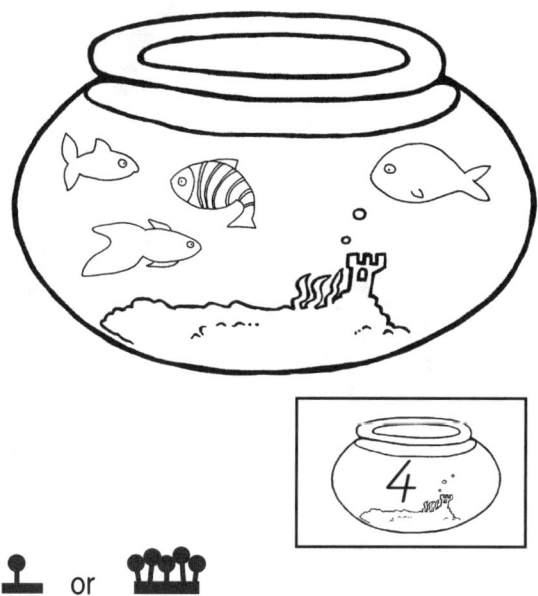

ONE or GROUP

•

Something Fishy

Work as a team.
Sort the fish into different bowls according to shape.
How many different types of fish are there?
How many fish in each bowl?
How did you sort the fish?
Is there any other way to sort them?

GROUP

• •

Fishy Patterns

Work with a partner.
Put the fish in a long line in a pattern.
Ask your partner what they think your pattern is. Swap roles.

Record one of your patterns on paper.

• •

Spin to 20

Play in teams of 3.
Use the 0-9 or 10-19 spinner.
Take turns to spin and place the matching number of fish into your team's bowl.
The winning team is the first team to get exactly 20 fish in their bowl.

Try to count on from the number you are at each turn.

• • •

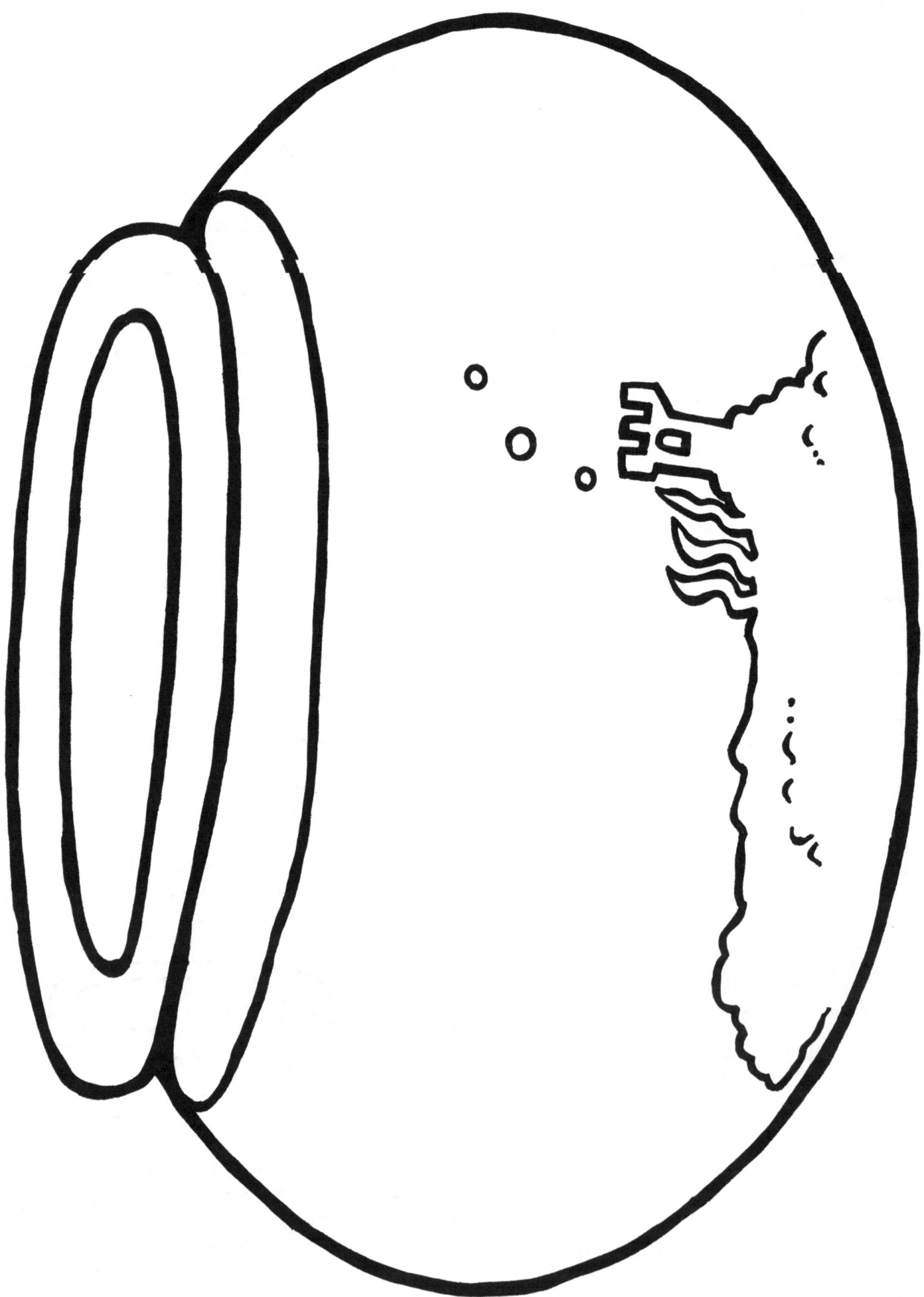

Hopping Frogs

Introducing the activity

Discuss how frogs live in ponds with lily pads. Frogs love to hop from one lily pad to another. The small cards show you how many frogs are on each lily pad at any one time.

Outcomes

Represents numerals using objects or drawings.
Counts collections up to 20.
Rote counts forwards to ...
Sorts and classifies objects into two or more sets.
Explains the sorting criterion for a given set.
Identifies similarities and differences in objects and sets.
Places objects into order by size, shape or number.
Demonstrates understanding of simple addition.
Records addition activities in their own way.

How to make the game

♦ If your budget doesn't stretch to 50 - 100 plastic frog counters, make four copies of the frog page. That will give you 60 frogs to start with. Colour the frogs, then laminate and cut out as separate frogs.

♦ Make 10 copies of the large lily pad page. Colour, laminate, then cut out each lily pad. Or, using a copy of the lily pad as a pattern, cut out 10 large lily pads from green felt.

♦ Make one copy of the 0 - 9 lily pad page. These are the activity cards that indicate how many frogs to put on each large lily pad. Laminate and cut into small rectangular cards.

♦ For extension activities, copy the 10 - 19 lily pad cards. Laminate and cut out. You will need at least another 50 frogs.

♦ Copy, laminate and cut out the four activity cards on the next page.

♦ Place all the equipment into a storage container and label clearly. Use the label provided on page 73.

Extra materials needed

Optional 50 - 100 plastic frog counters.
1 minute timer.

Hopping Frogs

Select a small card and place the matching number of frogs onto a large lily pad.
Use a timer and see how many lily pads you can match in 1 minute.

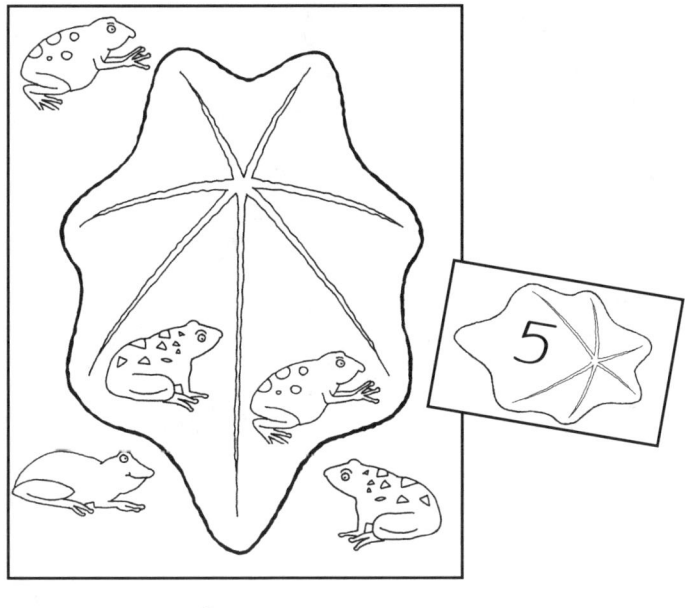

ONE or GROUP

•

All Sorts of Frogs

Sort the frogs onto different lily pads according to shape.
How many different types of frog are there?
How many frogs on each lily pad?
How did you sort the frogs?
Is there any other way to sort them?

PAIR or GROUP

• •

Collecting Frogs

Use the 0-6 die and 3 players. Take turns to throw the die and collect the matching number of frogs on your lily pad. How many frogs did you collect after 3 turns? Guess first, then check.

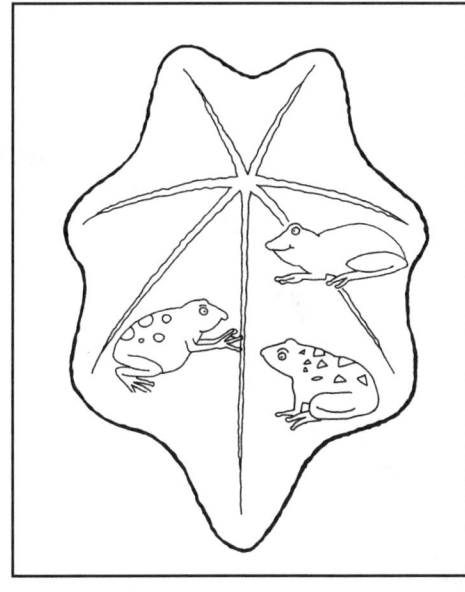

Who has the most frogs? The least? The same number as you?

GROUP

• •

Secret Frogs

Work with a partner. Arrange a secret number of frogs on your lily pad.
Show them to each other for about 2 seconds then hide them again.
Guess whether you both have the same, more or fewer frogs than each other.
Check, then repeat. Do your guesses get closer each time?

Make up a story to match one of your actions. Record this on paper.

ONE or GROUP

• • •

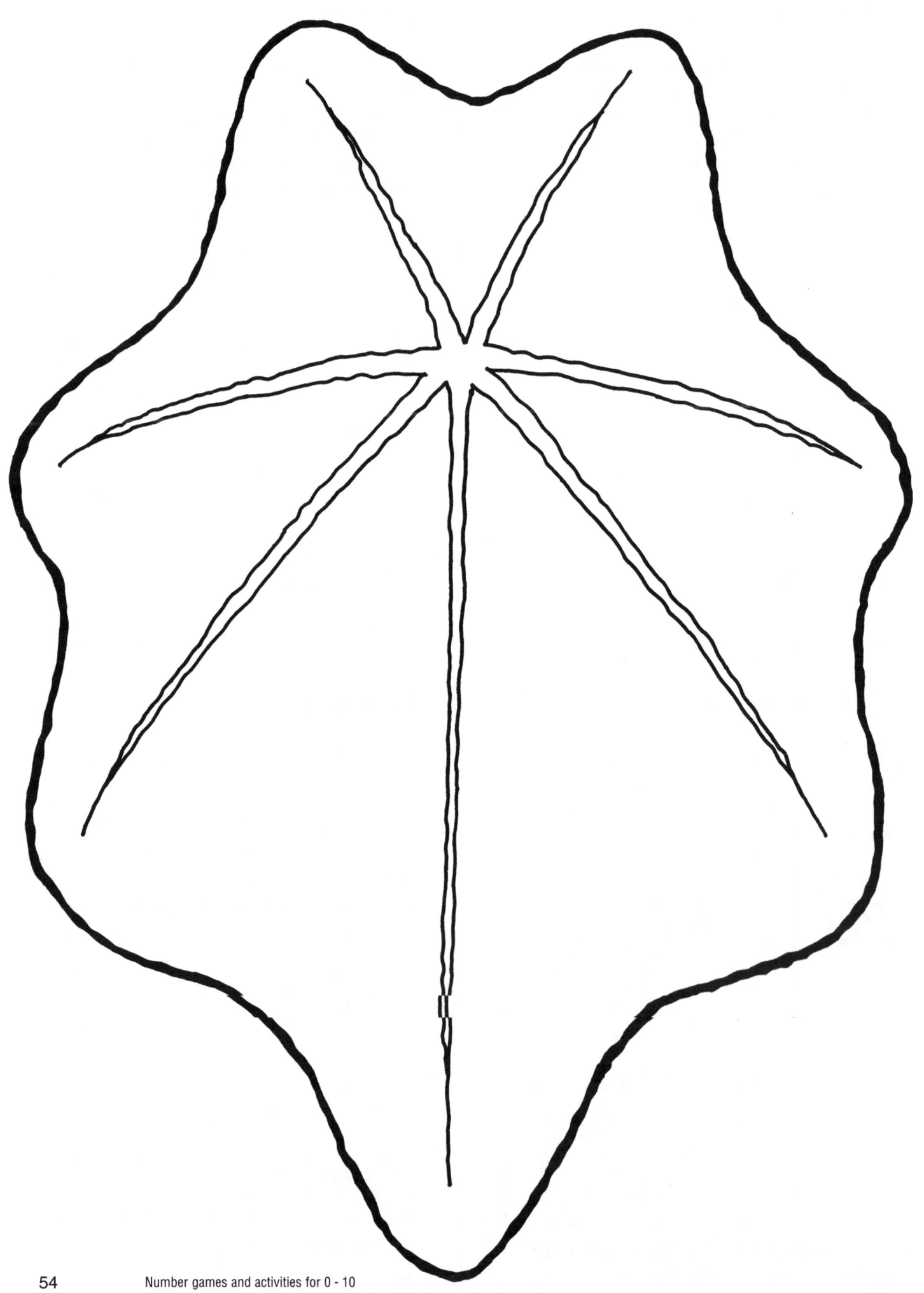

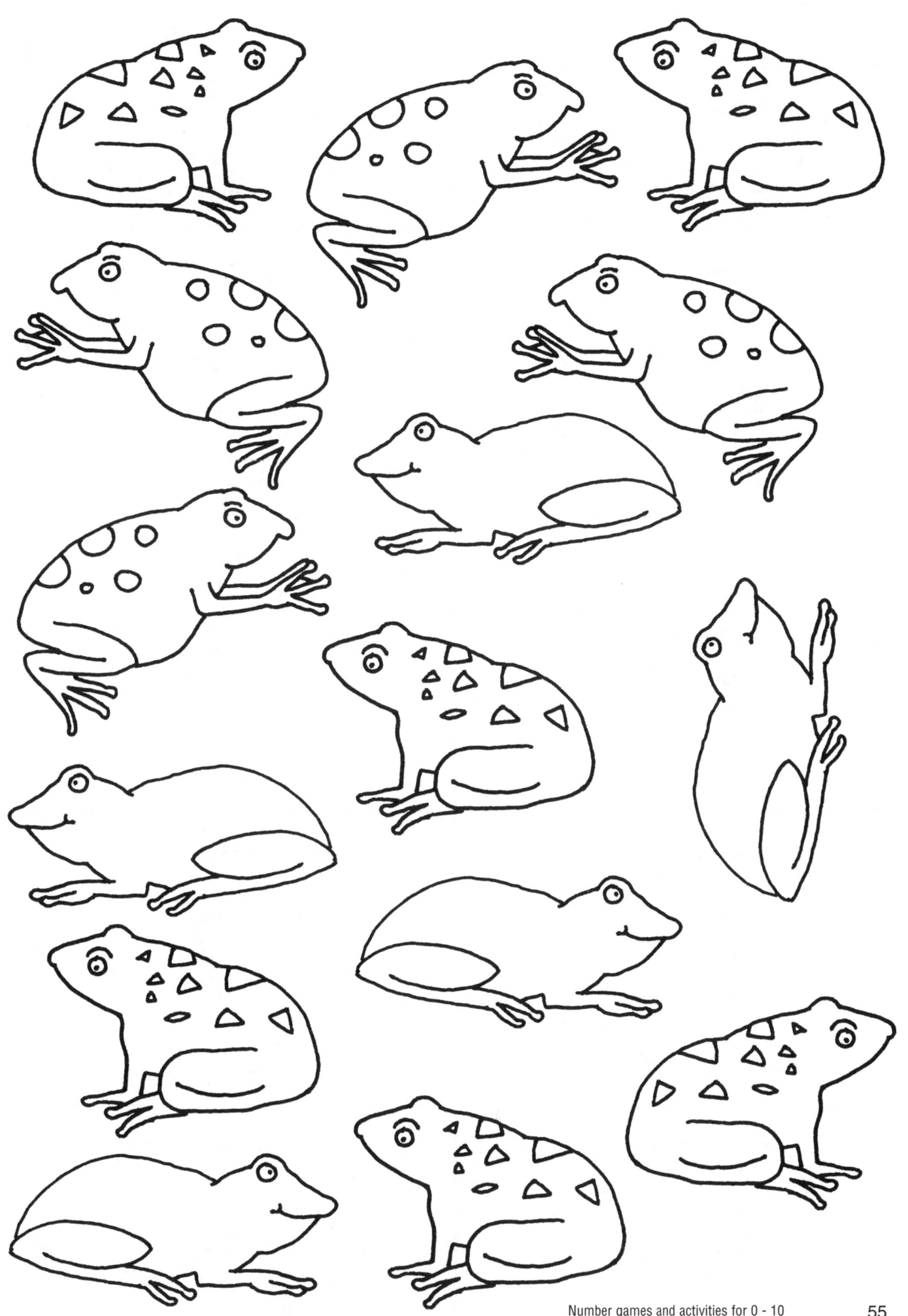

Number games and activities for 0 - 10

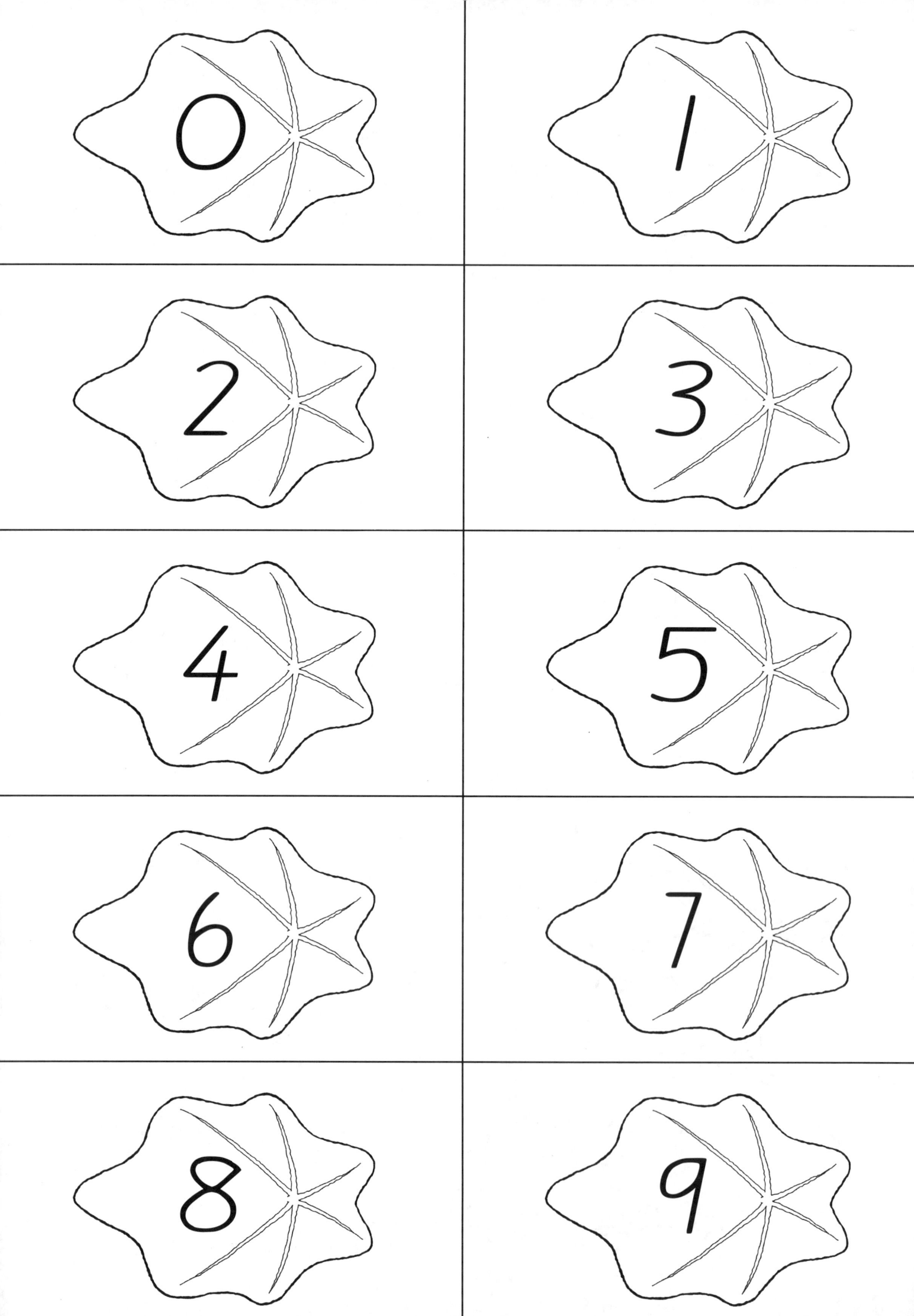

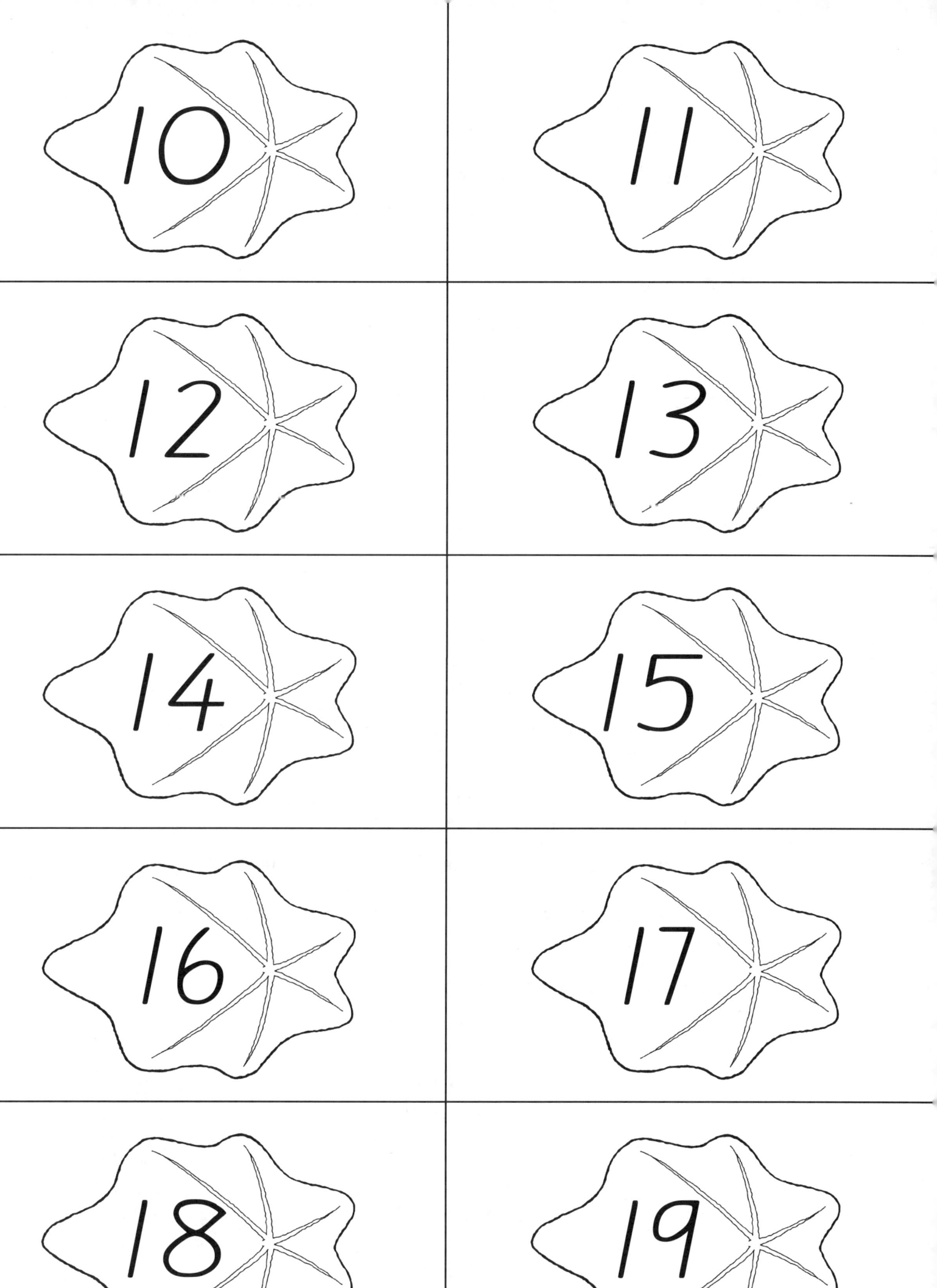

Freckles

Introducing the activity

Discuss how some people have a lot of freckles. Pretend that the counters are freckles.

Outcomes

Represents numerals using objects or drawings.
Counts collections up to ten or twenty.
Places objects into order by size, shape or number.
Rote counts forwards to ...
Rote counts backwards from...
Identifies missing numbers in a counting pattern.
Demonstrates understanding of simple subtraction.

How to make the game

♦ Make 10 copies of the large 'Freckles' face page. Colour and laminate.

♦ Make one copy of the Freckles 0 - 9 page. These are the activity cards which indicate how many measles to place on each face. Laminate and cut as individual cards.

♦ Make one copy of the 'Freckles' number word cards - zero to nine. Use these in place of the 0 - 9 cards at times.

♦ For extension activities, copy the 10 - 19 Freckles cards as well. Laminate and cut out. You will need to add plenty more counters.

♦ Copy, laminate and cut out the four activity cards on the next page.

♦ Place all the equipment into a storage container and label clearly. Use the label provided on page 73.

Extra materials needed

50-100 small plastic counters (10 mm diameter).

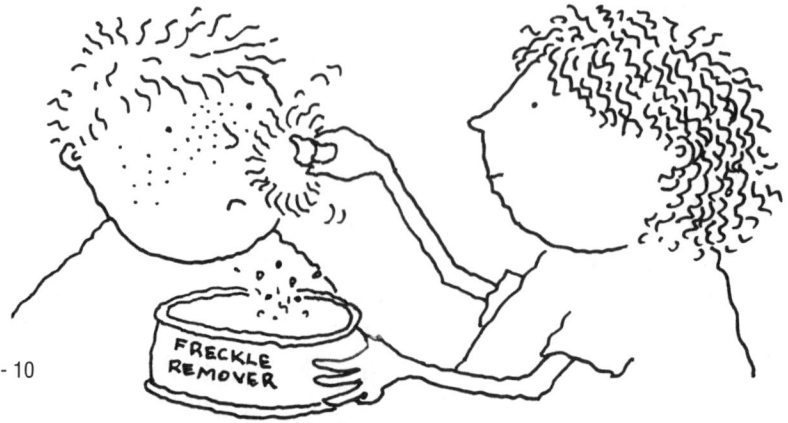

Freckles

Take a large face card and a small face card. Collect the matching number of counters and place on your face card.

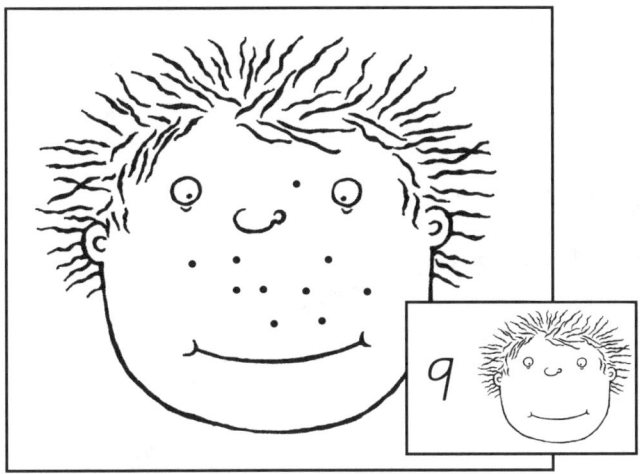

Make another face with more spots.
Make another face with fewer spots.
Make another face with the same number of spots.

 or   •

Missing Freckles

Put the small face cards into counting order forwards or backwards.
Remove some cards and ask your partner to name the missing numbers.
Swap roles.

PAIR   • •

Fewest to Most

Make up all the faces. Ask your partner to sort the faces into order from the fewest spots to the most spots. Place the matching set of number word cards under each face.

PAIR   • •

The Most Spots

Take 2 large face cards and a handful of spots. Count the spots and then share them between the faces. Is there a fair share? Repeat.

Try using 3 faces too!

PAIR   • • •

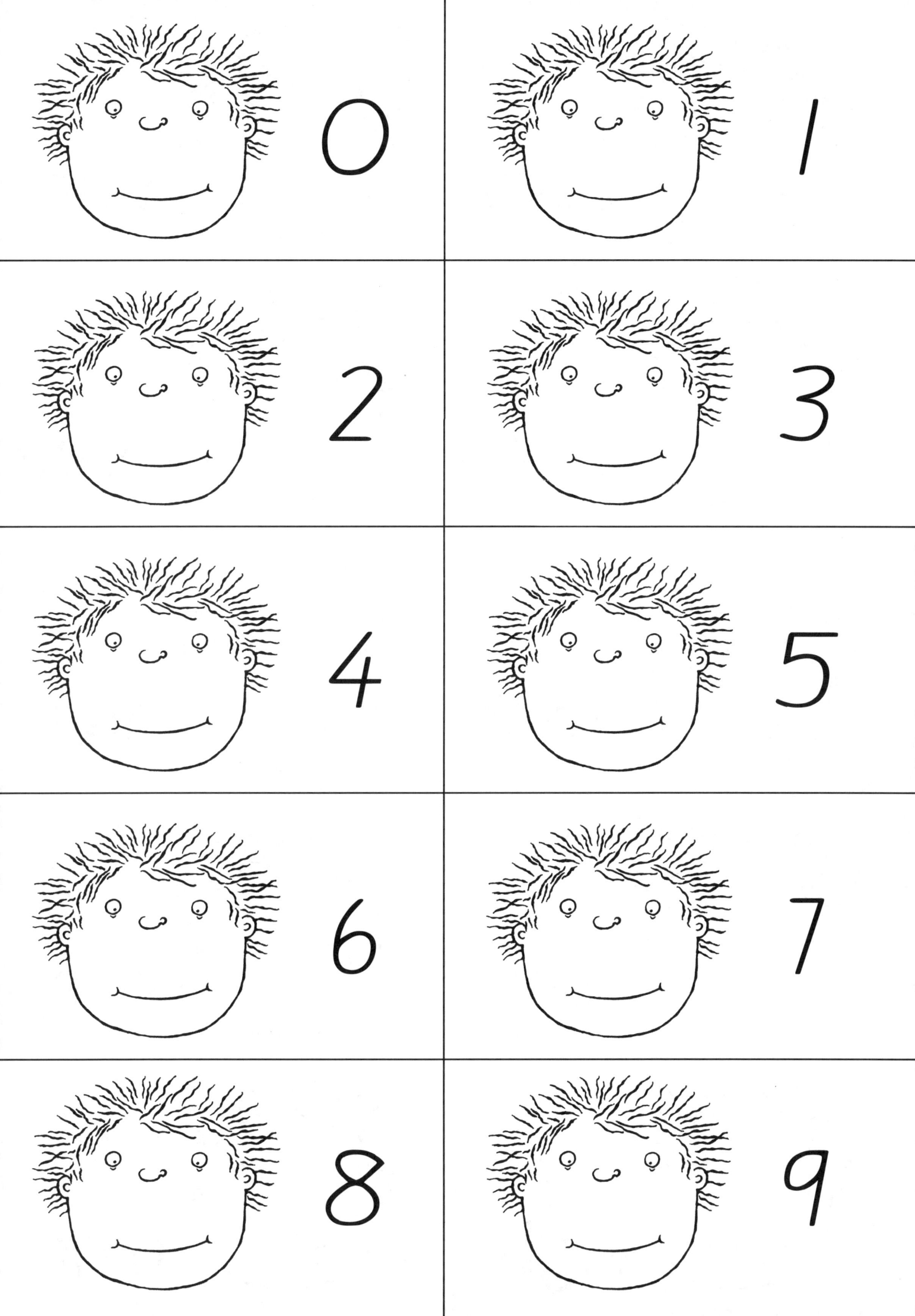

Busy Bees

Introducing the activity

Bees love to collect nectar from all the flowers in their territory. These bees are busy all day moving in and out of their beehives. The small cards show you how many bees are around the hive at any one time.

Outcomes

Compares and orders sets of objects using one-to-one correspondence.
Represents numerals using objects or drawings.
Counts collections up to ten or twenty.
Places objects into order by size, shape or number.
Identifies and continues a given pattern.
Records patterns by writing or drawing.
Creates their own counting patterns.
Demonstrates understanding of simple addition and subtraction.

How to make the game

♦ Make 10 copies of the large beehive. Colour each beehive and laminate.

♦ Make 3 copies of the Bees page. Colour in, laminate and cut out the individual bees.

♦ Make one copy of the 0 - 9 beehive page. These are the activity cards which indicate how many bees to place on each beehive. Laminate and cut out as individual cards.

♦ For extension activities, copy the 10 - 19 beehive cards as well. Laminate and cut out. You will need to add plenty more bees.

♦ Copy, laminate and cut out the eight activity cards on the next two pages.

♦ Place all the equipment into a storage container and label clearly. Use the label provided on page 73.

Extra materials needed

None.

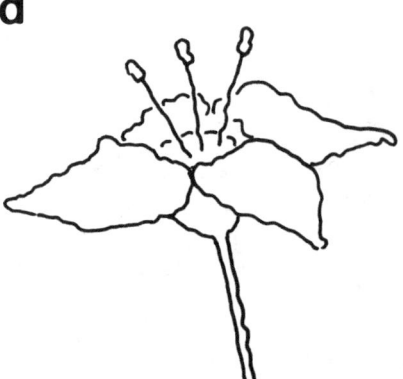

Home to the Beehive

Take a large beehive card and a small beehive card. Collect the matching number of bees and place them on your beehive. Make up a story to match.

Who has the most bees?
Who has the fewest bees?

GROUP

Patterns of Bees

Make a pattern using a handful of bees. Ask a friend to continue the pattern. Swap roles.

PAIR or GROUP

Busy Bees

Work with a partner. Give your partner instructions for placing bees on their hive, eg. Put 3 bees on the left and two on the right. Make one with 2 fewer bees than me.

Swap roles.

PAIR

Two beehives

Count up all the bees on 2 hives. Find a card which shows you how many altogether.

GROUP

Match the Number

Place some bees around your large beehive.
Count them. Turn over a small beehive card.
Add or take away bees to match the
new number.

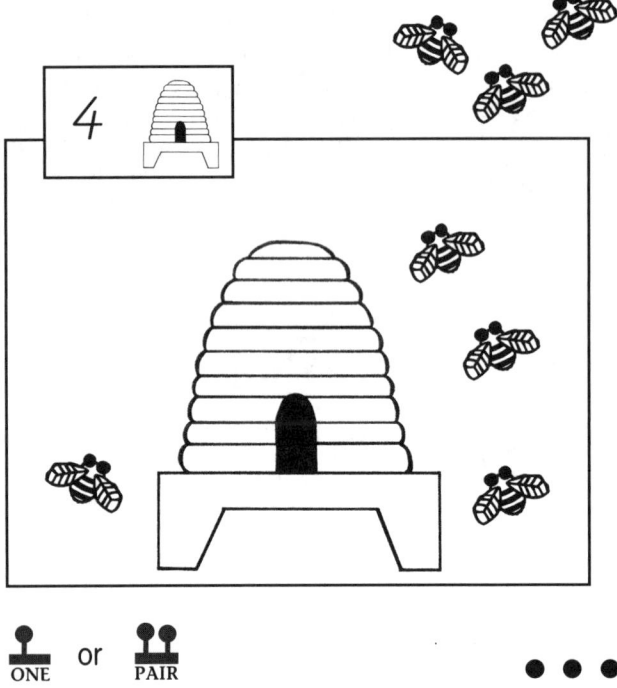

ONE or PAIR

20 Bees

Each team of 4 has a large beehive.
Take turns to throw the die and collect the
matching number of bees.
The team wins who collect exactly 20 bees.

GROUP

Bees fly away

Each team of 4 has a large beehive and
20 bees. Take turns to throw the die and take
away that number of bees. Try to be the first
team to have no bees at all.

GROUP

A Game for 2

Make up your own game for 2 players.

PAIR

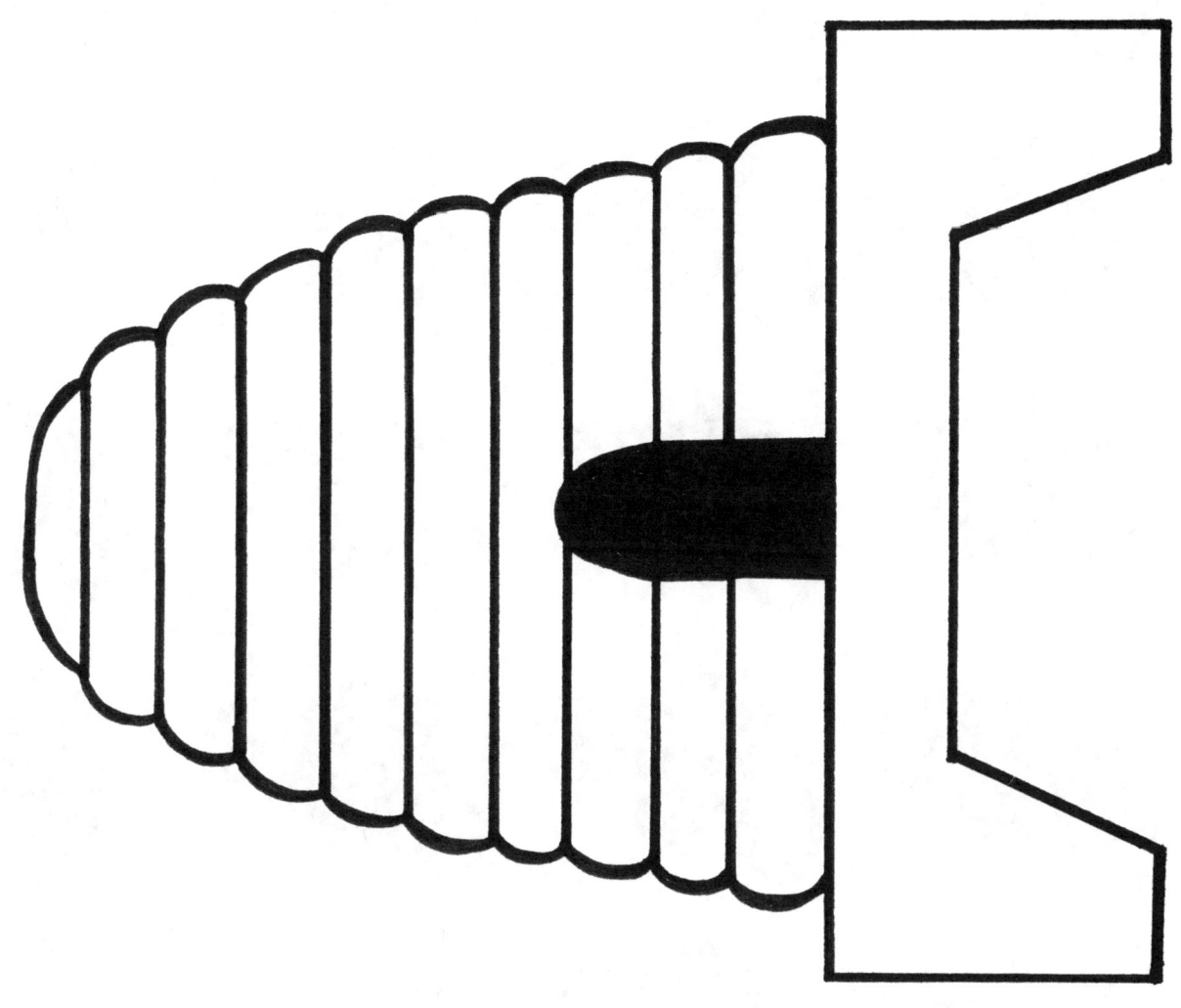

Bees

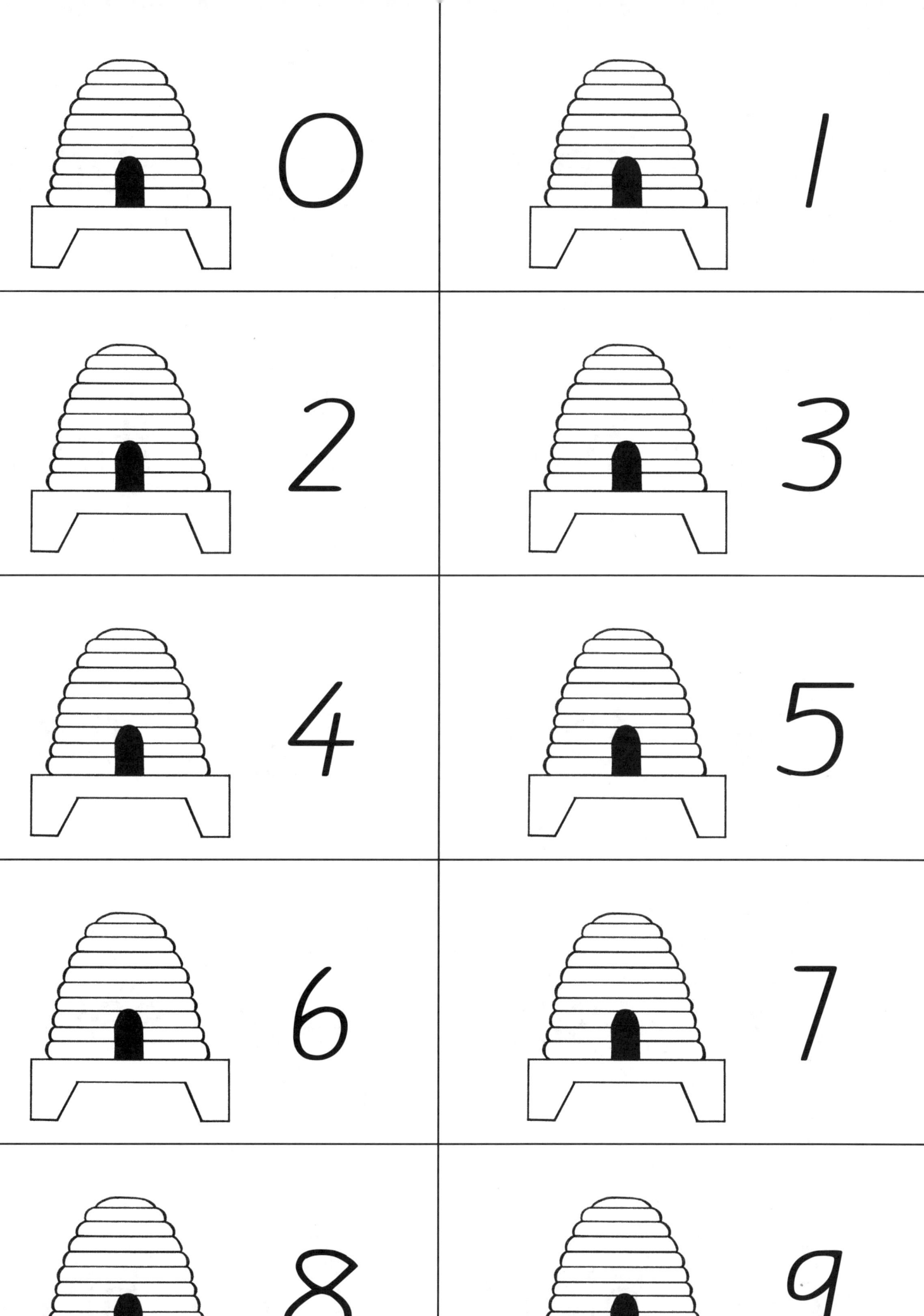

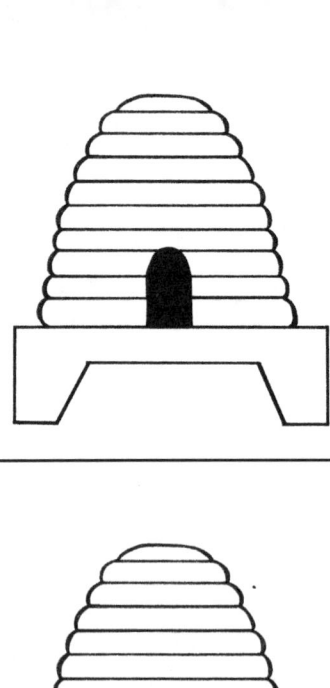 zero | 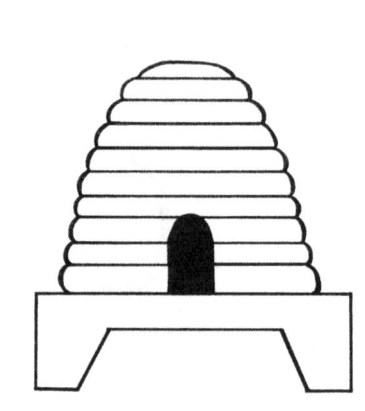 one

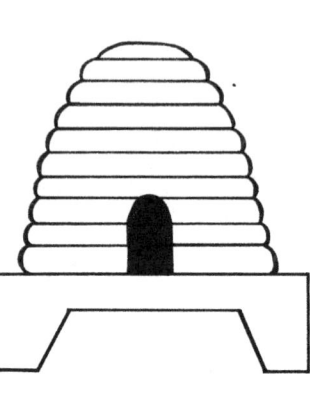 two | 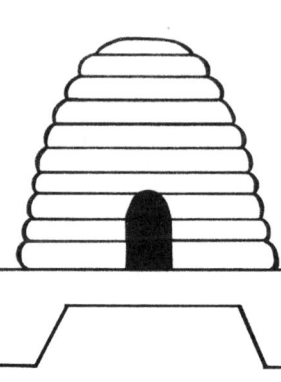 three

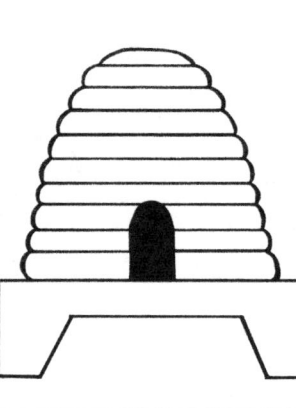 four | 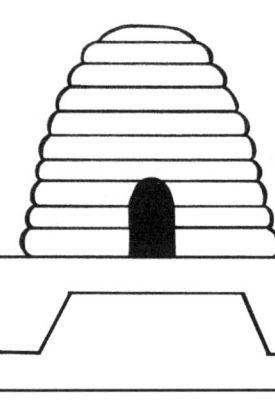 five

 six | 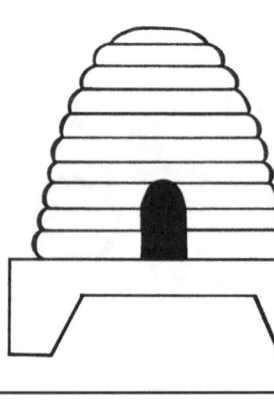 seven

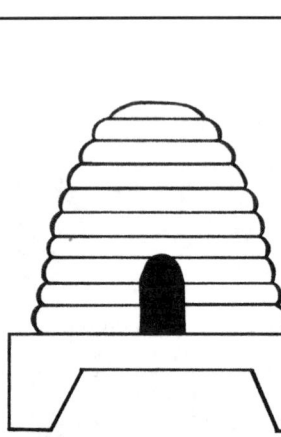 eight | 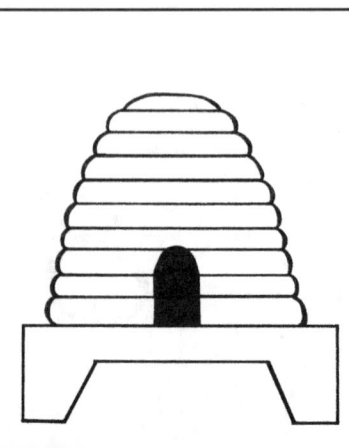 nine

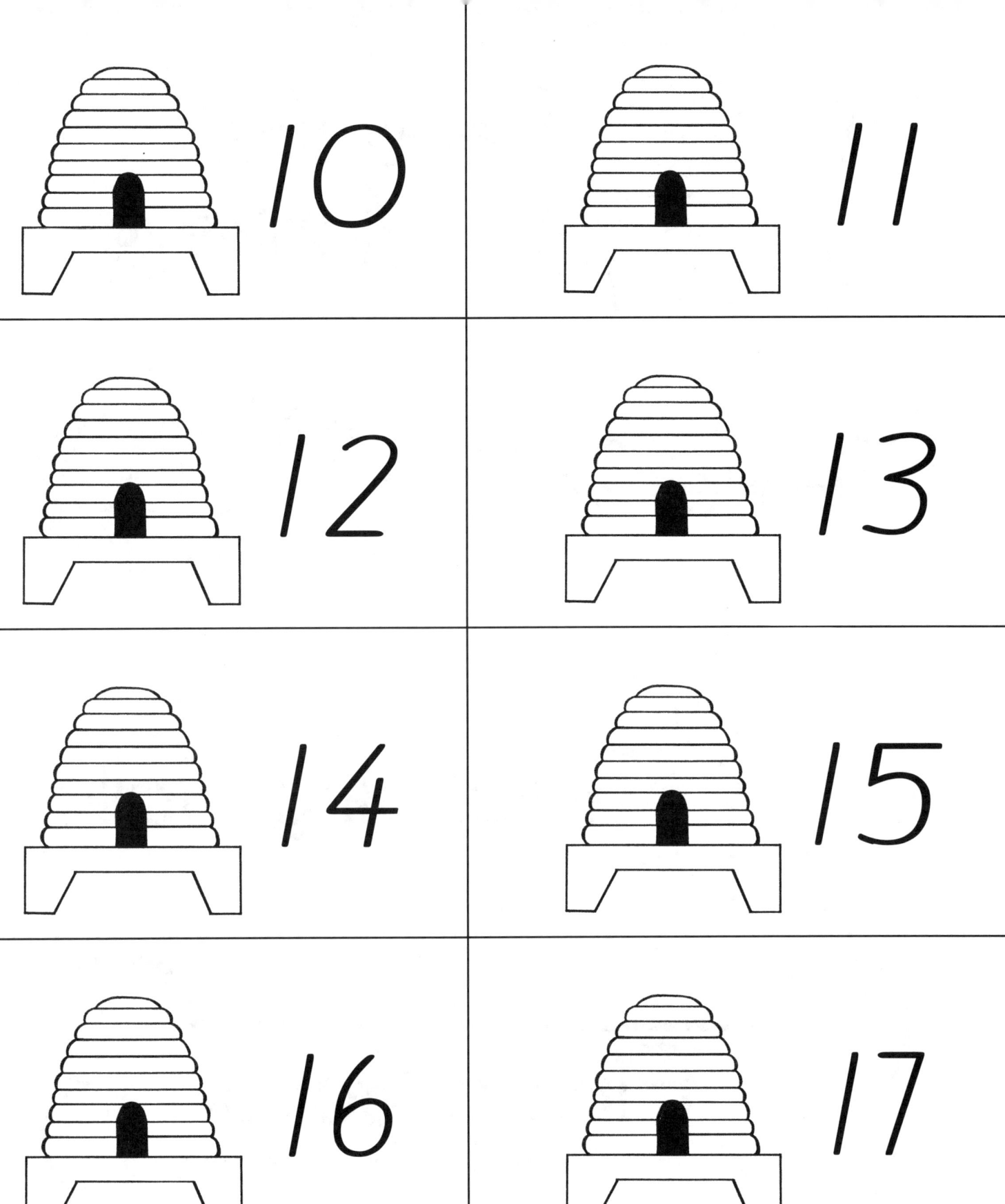

Feed the Monkeys

Zebra Stripes

Balancing Balls

Find a Bone

How Hairy?

Set the Table

Something Fishy

Hopping Frogs

Freckles

Busy Bees

Net for a 1 - 6 Die (Dots)

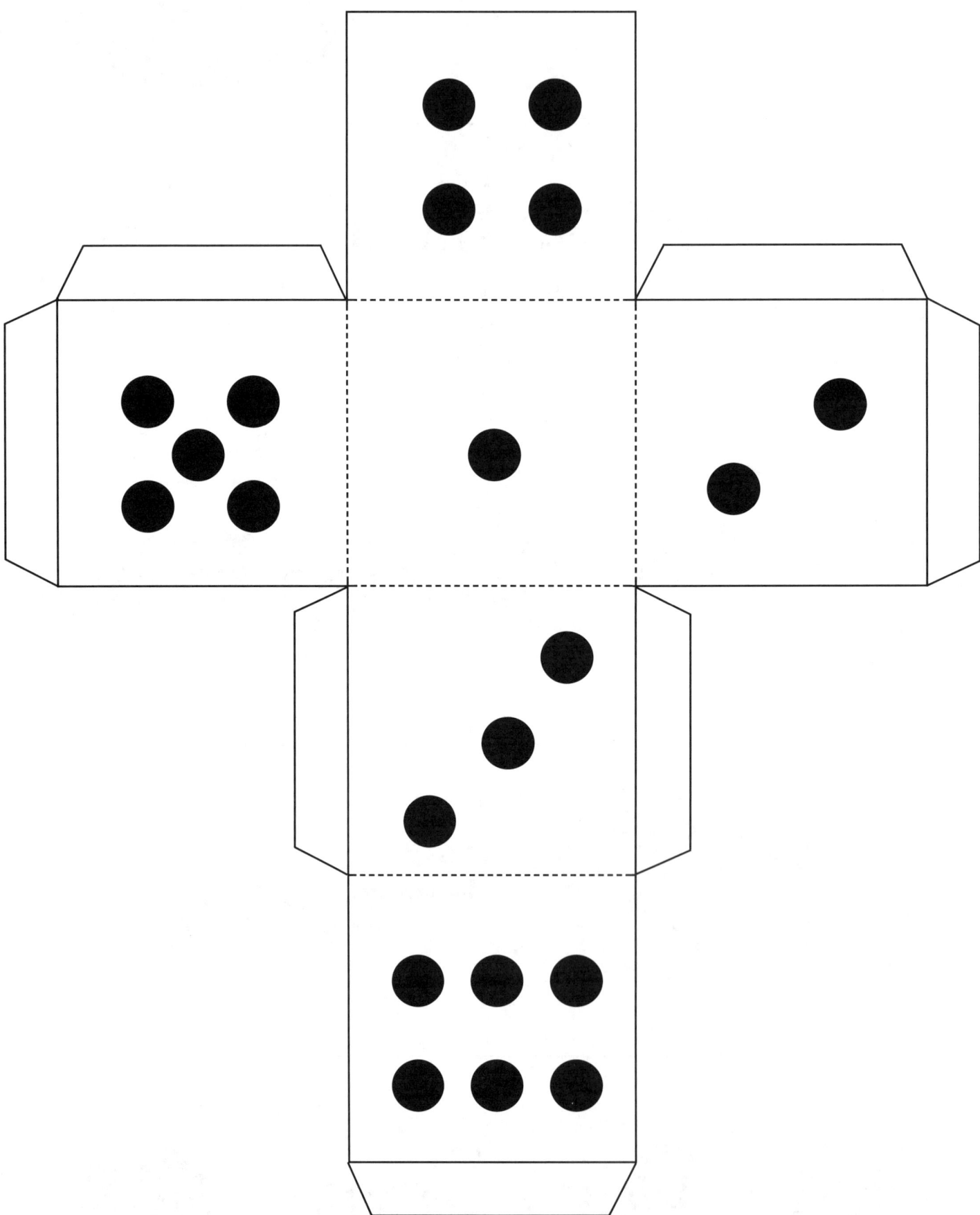

Net for a 1 - 6 Die (Numerals)

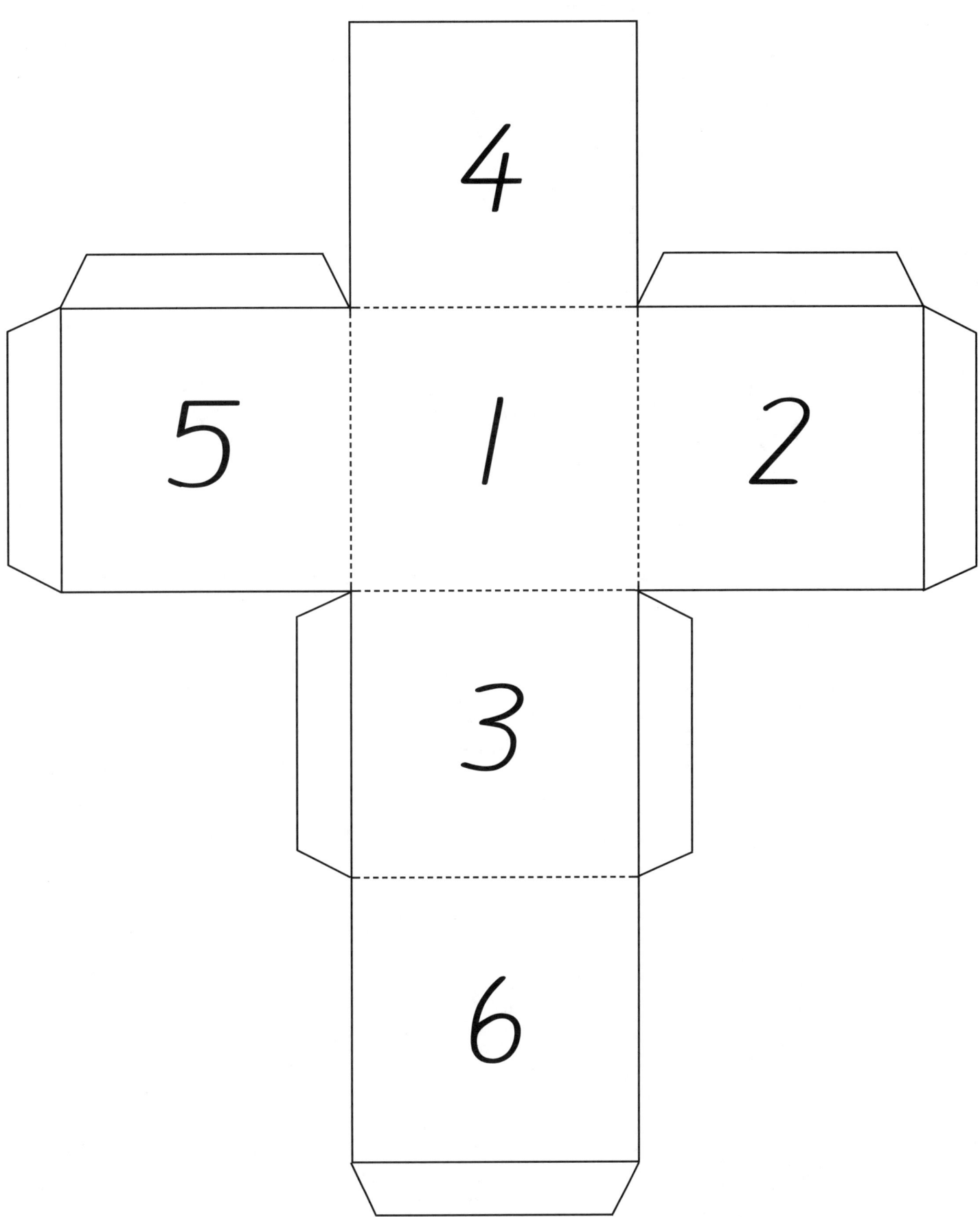

Number games and activities for 0 - 10

Net for a 7 - 12 Die (Numerals)

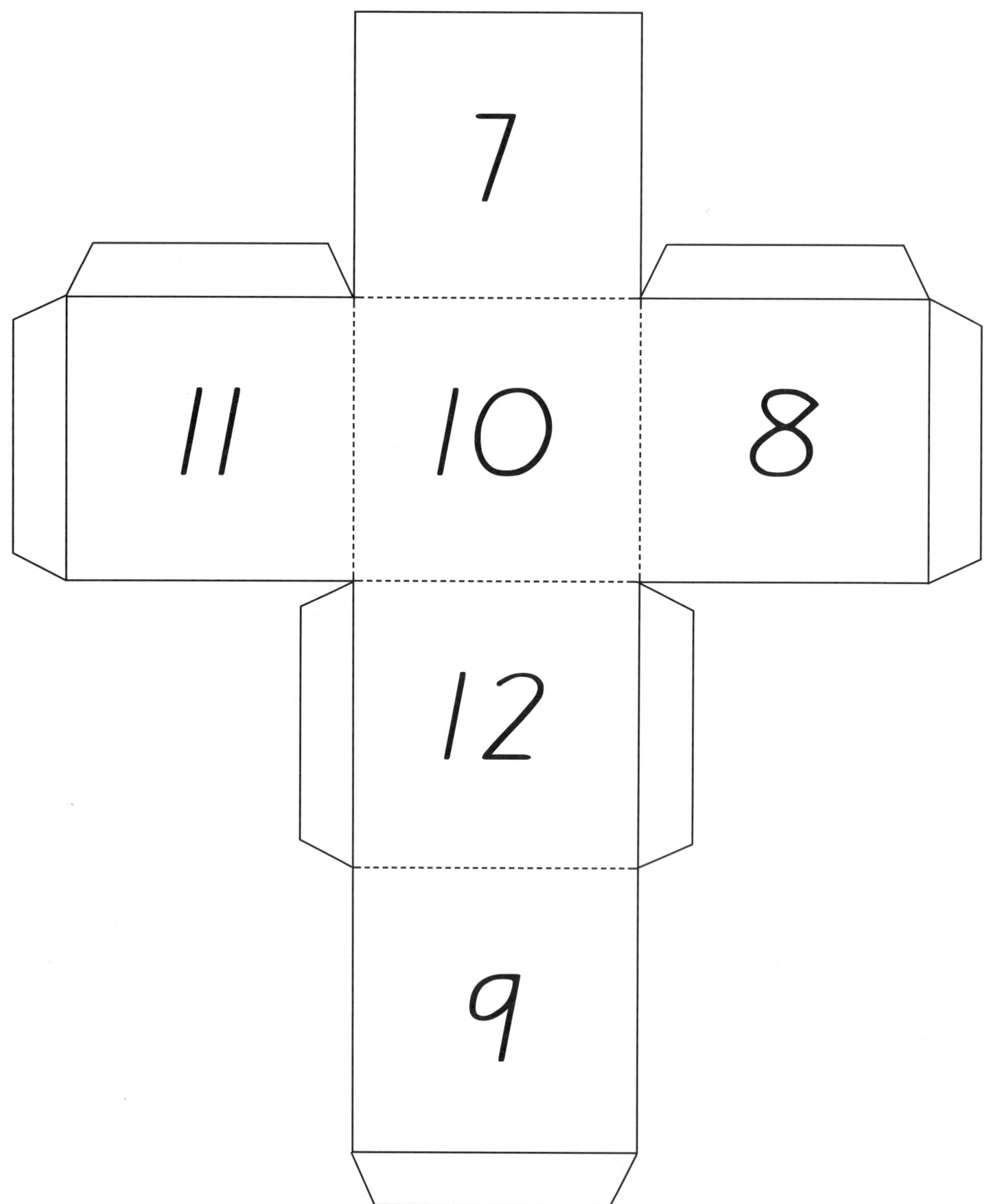

Spinners 0 – 9

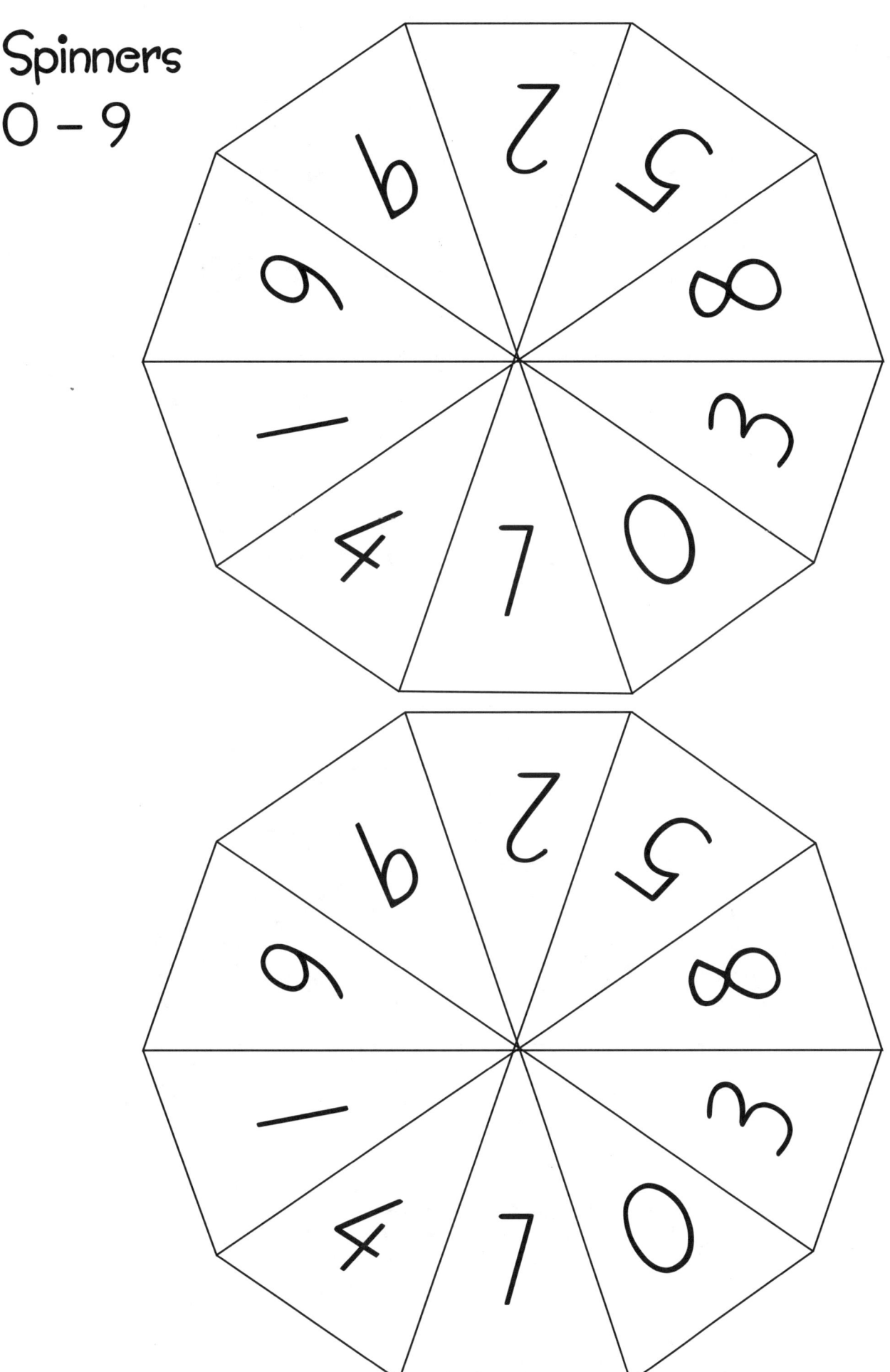

Number games and activities for 0 - 10

Spinners 10 - 19

Number games and activities for 0 - 10